Galloping Jones was a bare-knuckle-fighting larrikin who could tame any horse. Moondyne Joe escaped prison using an ingenious plan that made a whole colony laugh. Caroline Coleman was a settler who raised her children in Western Queensland, and buried her husband behind the store they built near the Thomson River.

Nemarluk was an Aboriginal freedom fighter, who roamed the Daly River region of the Northern Territory.

Based on the popular Stories of Oz history posts, these sketches of Australia's past will inform and entertain you. Above all, they will remind you of what life was like, in the days before highways and smart phones.

Also by Greg Barron

HarperCollins Publishers Australia

Rotten Gods
Savage Tide
Lethal Sky
Voodoo Dawn (short fiction)

Stories of Oz Publishing

The Hammer of Ramenskoye (short fiction)
Camp Leichhardt
Galloping Jones and Other True Stories from Australia's History
Whistler's Bones
Red Jack and the Ragged Thirteen
Outlaw: The Story of Joe Flick
The Time of Thunder

Galloping Jones
and other True Stories from Australia's History

Second Edition

Greg Barron

Stories of Oz Publishing

Second edition published 2020 by Stories of Oz Publishing
PO Box K57
Haymarket NSW 1240
ABN: 0920230558
facebook.com/storiesofoz
ozbookstore.com

The right of Greg Barron to be identified as the author of this work has been asserted by him in accordance with the Copyright Amendment (Moral Rights) Act 2000

This work is copyright. Apart from any use as permitted under the Copyright Act 1968, no part may be reproduced, copied, scanned, stored in a retrieval system, recorded, or transmitted, in any form or by any means, without the prior written permission of the publisher.

© 2020 Greg Barron
ISBN: 978 0 6480627 3 8
Proof reading: Robert Barron
Cover design: PixelStudio and James Barron.
Cover Photography: Scott Higgins
Typeset by Stories of Oz

Table of Contents

Galloping Jones	10
Ben Hall	13
Charlie Flannigan and the Auvergne Station Murder	16
The Ballad of Tom Coolon	21
The Ragged Thirteen: 'Tea and Sugar' Bushrangers	30
The Eulo Queen	36
The Katherine Terrace	39
Gunman	39
Nemarluk the Outlaw	42
James 'Jimmy' Darcy	46
The Tragedy of Joe Flick	49
Captain Moonlite	54
The JC	58
Augusta Marion Gaunt	60
Catherine Coleman	64
The 'Petticoat' Drovers	67
Pearling on the Mona	85
The Leviathan	88
Lost	90
The Lake Nash Drought and a Push for Water	92
The Man with a Mission	97
The Town on the Flood Plain	102
John Moore Gaunt and the St Kilda Years	104
The Girder that Wouldn't Fit	111
The McGree Brothers of Taylors Arm	114
The Nackeroos	117
The Stone-throwing Battle of the Margaret River	119
The Siege of Dagworth	121
The Battle of Long Tan	124
Bennelong	129
So who the hell was Alice anyway?	132
Paddy Cahill	136
Buckley's Chance	138

Making Fools of the Law	141
Tom Turner, Pine Creek Cop	144
The Capture of the Kenniff Brothers	148
Moondyne Joe	151
Harry Readford	153
Collateral Damage	159
Mary Watson of Lizard Island	161
Assisted Immigration	164
Barbara of the Kaurareg	166
Charlotte Badger	168
The Ethel Pirates	170
The Wreck of the Tryal	173
Gold Rush on the Palmer River	176
The Big Australian	182
The Opalton Heist	184
Territory Gold	186
The Loaded Dog	200
Elizabeth Woolcock	203
Alma McGee	213
Steele Rudd	217
Where the Dead Men Lie	221
Edward Dickens	225
Jack and Kate	227
Nat Buchanan	235
Captain Joe Bradshaw	239
Carrie Creaghe	243
Charles Fisher	245
Sixty Ships and One Thousand Men.	248
The Marion Sleigh	250
The Providence	252

CHARACTERS AND KILLERS

Galloping Jones

Queensland has produced a character or two over the years, but John Decy 'Galloping' Jones takes some beating. Apart from being one of the most talented rough riders of his generation, and one hell of a bare-knuckle fighter, he was famously light-fingered.

Galloping Jones got his nickname from a horse race where he and his mates prepared a ring-in. Apart from boot polish cunningly applied to a white blaze, part of the trick was to make the substitute's tail longer. Unfortunately the glue they used to fix the tail extensions started melting half way through the race. The crowd noticed pretty quickly. Jones and his mount reached the finish line ahead of the pack, but rather than face the stewards he just kept on galloping, through the gates and into the bush.

One night Jones complained that when he walked into a pub everyone left.

'I don't leave,' said a voice. Jones turned to see a big bloke called Treacle MacFarlane walking towards him.

'And why don't you leave, Treacle?'

'Because I can fight just as well as you can.'

Legend has it that they fought for two hours before the bout was declared a draw.

No one could best Jones on a horse, and his freakish ability to stay in the saddle saw him recruited to Lance Skuthorpe's famous travelling show. Jones's fame at riding buckjumpers was such that he would ride into town and dare locals to bring out their worst horses just so he could tame them. More than once, if he liked the horse, he lived up to his name and just kept on galloping.

According to the Queenslander newspaper:

> *'Galloping' Jones has established the fact that he is a master horseman, and he is recognised as such today. As a horseman and stockman he is recognised as one of the central figures of the Gulf districts. He could be relied on to tame any horse that any other man had failed with, and while he may not quieten him sufficient for any ordinary rider he would never be thrown himself.*

Jones joined the AIF in World War One and came back with even less regard for authority than when he left. Police gazettes list charges against him for assault, creating a disturbance and using obscene language. He robbed at least one bank and was shot in the shoulder for resisting arrest. He was known to steal, sell, and then re-steal the same cattle on the same day.

Another time, arrested for horse theft, he asked his captors for permission to head behind a bush for a 'call of nature.' When they went looking for him Jones had run off, but recapturing him wasn't hard. The police found him at the nearest pub.

Even past his prime, Jones was not afraid to stick his neck out. In 1926 the Northern Herald Newspaper carried a challenge from Jones to a boxer called Bob Smith to take him on for a prize of £25. The paper noted that, 'Promoter Bob Ditton said that when he presented the agreements to Smith last night the latter seemed unwilling to meet Jones.'

One year later Jones appeared before the police magistrate in Rockhampton, charged with 'using obscene language in a public place, assaulting Constable WH Langhorne whilst in execution of his duty, and resisting arrest.'

There's a sad side to all this. Jones married later in life and had three children. The relationship didn't work out, and he was often in trouble for failing to provide maintenance payments. He was a free spirit, and couldn't stick to anything for long. That must have been hard on his family.

As an old man, at Eventide nursing home in Charters Towers, Galloping Jones continued to cause trouble – fighting, getting drunk and wandering off to the pub. He died in 1959, 66 years old, of heart disease and emphysema.

Ben Hall

The word bushranger is a uniquely Australian term for the lawless characters who roamed the fringes of civilised districts seeking easy money through robbery and violence. The word was first used in the Sydney Gazette in 1805, referring to a wild assortment of escaped convicts, deserters from the military and disillusioned free immigrants; full-bearded, dirty, and afraid of nothing.

The gold rushes of the 1850s saw the heyday of these bushrangers, but they had pretty much disappeared by the late 1880s as better police tactics, technology and burgeoning population made it harder for them to hide out in the bush for the long periods necessary.

The most famous bushranger was certainly Ned Kelly, but Captain Thunderbolt, John Gilbert, and Frank Gardiner are still well-known. Most interesting of them all, perhaps, was Ben Hall, who became a bushranger for reasons of passion, not lust for wealth or an easy life.

Ben was working as a stockman just out of Forbes, New South Wales, and was strong, reliable and honest. He had no time for bushrangers or dishonesty of any sort, and soon saved enough money to buy a small place of his own.

He married a local girl called Bridget in 1856, but she proved not to return Ben's steadfast love and loyalty. Falling in love with a flash young stockman, she took hers and Ben's child to be with her lover. Ben was heartbroken, but that wasn't the end of it. When she was seduced and bedded by a policeman Ben swore vengeance on that 'trap' and all his kind. Ben Hall took to the bush he knew so well, the remote Wedden Mountains, and became one of the most feared men of his generation.

Despite this reputation, he robbed only from the rich, mainly mail coaches with their rich burden of gold. According to folklore Ben Hall never killed a man, right up to that fateful day in 1865, when police found him alone at his campsite at Billabong Creek.

According to the testimony of one of the policemen, Sub-inspector James Henry Davidson:

> I levelled a double-barrelled gun and fired one shot. I believe I hit him, for he halted and looked back. Sergeant Condell and Billy then fired. I think they both hit him; we fired pretty close together.
>
> Condell and Billy were running a little in my rear, about fifteen yards to my left; Hall ran about sixty yards to a few saplings, and caught hold of one. I think he was then mortally wounded. The four constables and tracker then came across. I think Hall saw them coming, for he changed his course; they fired; I was then within thirty yards, when Hipkiss fired his revolving rifle.
>
> I noticed Hall's revolver belt fall to the ground. Hall, still holding to the sapling, gradually fell back; altogether, thirty shots were fired. Several were fired after Hipkiss fired; I fancy he was

shot in the head after that. He spoke afterwards. He said, 'I'm wounded, shoot me dead.'

When they carried Ben Hall's corpse into Forbes he had nine bullet wounds, four of which might have been fatal.

Charlie Flannigan and the Auvergne Station Murder

September 1892. The game was cribbage for a stick of tobacco each hand. Four men whiling away a long night by the light of a slush lamp on Auvergne Station, near the NT/WA border. Even today, Auvergne is an isolated and dramatic locale; rugged mountains cut through by the Bullo, Baines and Victoria Rivers.

Among the men playing cards in a lean-to behind the kitchen that night was Sam Croker, the acting manager. Croker was an experienced stockman, having arrived in the Territory droving a mob of breeders from Queensland to Wave Hill Station for Nat Buchanan. A stockman called McPhee and a Chinese cook, Joe Ah Wah, were also at the table.

Another man playing cards that day was an Aboriginal stockman called Charlie Flannigan, also called McManus. Charlie had been raised by his white father in the Richmond Downs area in Queensland, and had also learned his trade with Nat Buchanan. He had arrived at Auvergne one week earlier, with just a horse, saddle, perhaps a few of the sketches of bush life he loved to draw, and a rifle.

Before the game started Joe Ah Wah told Flannigan that he didn't feel like a game that night.

'Best you play now,' said Flannigan bluntly. 'For you can't

play cards when you are dead.' Joe agreed to play a couple of hands, and when they cut the cards to choose partners, Ah Wah and Flannigan teamed up.

Some reports of what followed cited an argument over the card game, but Joe Ah Wah's testimony did not mention it. According to Joe, part way through the evening, Flannigan took a drink of water from a cask, then went out to the shed in which the men slept, a crude structure of poles with branches piled over the top. He came back carrying his rifle.

Taking up position at a tree near the lean-to, Flannigan raised the rifle to his shoulder and aimed it at Croker. The men at the table were oblivious to what was about to happen.

This, it has to be said, was not the first or last time violence had boiled over at Auvergne. The station had a chequered history in those days. As Charlie Gaunt later wrote:

In recording sketches of the olden days I cannot pass Auvergne Station on the Baines River, where more tragedies have been enacted than any station in the North.

I was stock-keeping on that station when Jack Skene was managing it. The manager before Skene, Hardy by name, was speared to death at the old station, down the Baines on the opposite side of the river from where the present station now stands. For years after you could see the stone spear head sticking inches in the door post where it passed through Hardy as he rushed through the door for his rifle.

But men weren't the only hazards on Auvergne, according to Charlie.

Alligators ... came up through the garden, tearing up pumpkin vines and into the beef house, once taking a quarter of beef off a hook.

Charlie went on to list a litany of tragedies, including more spearings, fatal riding accidents and murder. Most bloody of all was the day Charlie Flannigan took aim at his boss part way through a game of cards.

Flannigan fired once, and Croker slid to the floor, mortally struck in the chest. According to the eyewitness report of Barney, a black stockman who was in the shed at the time, Croker called out 'I am dead,' after being shot the first time.

Flannigan walked up and finished Croker off with a second round to the head.

Joe ah Wah ran off into the bush, while McPhee helped Charlie wrap his victim in a blanket. Thirty-six tense hours with Flannigan in control of the station followed. Fearing reprisal he searched for and confiscated any firearms. He also forced the others to help bury Croker's body.

Sketches by Charlie Flannigan (Photo courtesy South Australian Museum)

So how did a normally inoffensive stockman come to commit murder? He was a good worker, generally popular, and loved to draw pictures.

Gordon Buchanan, who worked with Flannigan on cattle drives as well as on Wave Hill Station, described him as "… a fair horseman and stockman, and an expert in the drafting yards and branding pen. Illiterate, but fairly well spoken, he seldom swore."

The key might be in something Flannigan said to Joe just after the shooting. "I have let him run long enough, six months now."

Also, the next day, viewing the bloody, blanket wrapped body, Flannigan appeared to address the dead man directly. "Well, old fellow, I've had the pleasure of sewing you up instead of you sewing me up"'

So if this killing was just a disagreement over a card game, why did Flannigan later tell Joe Ah Wah that he had waited six months to kill Croker. Was this the result of a long-running vendetta? On the other hand, if there was an open grudge between the two men, why would Croker have allowed Flannigan onto the station. Let alone given him a job. The answer, it seems, is lost to history.

In any case, within two days of the murder, Flannigan extorted a cheque for his "wages" from McPhee and rode hard for the Western Australian border.

Friends at Ord River Station, however, convinced Charlie to give himself up in Hall's Creek. Burdened by manacles that weighed close to ten kilograms, he was taken on horseback to Wyndham, then on the steamer, Rob Roy, to Palmerston.

In prison, Charlie had the time and the materials to pursue his love of drawing. He sketched sad images of the bush, the things he had seen. Even though he was illiterate, Flannigan copied words and letters, and some of his pictures seem to spell out words. He drew stockmen and steamers, homesteads and bush scenes. The full collection of these sketches is now held by the South Australian museum.

A newspaper article described how white man's justice was served on Flannigan, the first man to be hanged in the Northern Territory

The execution of Charlie Flanagan took place at the Fannie Bay Labour Prison

at 9 o'clock to-day. Since his conviction the prisoner had maintained a cool demeanour throughout. His chief expressed desire was that he should not show the white feather. Although admitting the crime for which he was sentenced, he showed no contrition or desire to avoid the death penalty. He slept well last night, and breakfasted and smoked this morning, and mounted the scaffold alone. The whole arrangements for the execution were carried through successfully, and death was instantaneous.

The Ballad of Tom Coolon

Thomas Cuthbert Coolon was born in Richmond, New South Wales, on the tenth of April 1859. His mother, Sarah Douglass, died when he was seven years old. His father remarried and moved out west of the Darling River where Tom was abducted by a group of Aborigines.

For the next decade Tom was raised by wild blacks, learning and honing bush skills that would become legendary. He also learned harsh laws of retribution and payback that would lead, later in life, to a shocking tragedy.

As squatters and their stock pushed further out into the scrub Tom found himself once more part of white society. With his lean frame and general toughness he quickly fell into station work. Some cattle stealing on the side saw a policeman ride out with an arrest warrant in Tom's name.

Tom, however, had the 'trap' in his sights long before he arrived, and shot the horse out from under him.

This, it seemed to Tom, was a good time to take a change of scenery up in Queensland, where he worked as a ringer, dog-baiter, and roo-shooter. In his spare time he developed an interest in prospecting. Tom was a striking looking man; tall with blue eyes and a blazing red beard. In 1890 he married Catherine Mongovan. The couple had two daughters and a son, living in the Clermont district, Queensland.

The turn of the century saw Tom droving with Ted Drewer up to the Territory, taking a mob of brood mares to one of the vast Fisher and Lyons properties. When the mares had been delivered he headed for Darwin, intending to take a ship home to Queensland. The wet season had struck early, rivers were flooded and impassable all the way down the Top End and across the Gulf country. Riding home would have been impossible.

THOS. COOLAN.

News hit Darwin of a droving camp near Newcastle Waters facing starvation and fever, cut off from the world. A desperate call went out for a volunteer to ride five hundred miles south with supplies for the stricken men.

Tom Coolon stepped forward, and with three riding horses and two packs he set out on a mission few men would have attempted.

Swimming the horses across flooded rivers he managed to cover an astonishing fifty miles each day. Sadly that perilous rescue mission came too late, for the last of the drovers died on the day Tom arrived.

Tom was now a legend in the Territory, but back in

Queensland things went bad. First, the Coolons' twelve-year-old daughter Mary died. Then Tom took up a partnership on a station called Prairie Run, near Clermont, but the business arrangement degenerated into a bitter feud that included the odd gunfight.

Tom and Catherine took up the adjoining property, Spoonbill Farm, but Tom's former partners, the Kirkups, were out to get him, framing him for the possession of stolen livestock, a 'crime' that saw him imprisoned for two years with hard labour. When he was released Tom Coolon was a changed man.

It was race day in Clermont when Tom came up against the law again. He was drinking at the pub when a stranger tried to pick a fight. The two men were shaping up when a huge policeman called Ormes banged their heads together and threw them against a wall.

Legend has it that Tom Coolon slowly stood up, then fixed his eyes on Constable Ormes. 'I won't forget this. It will be evened up.'

When, a few months later, the policeman's corpse was found at a place called Camp Oven Hole on the Charters Towers Road, Tom was naturally a suspect.

From a recollection in the Townsville Bulletin:

> *It was in that country later that Constable Ormes was shot at the 33 Mile, better known as Camp Oven Waterhole, on the Clermont-Charters Towers Road. The head of Ormes's horse was still hanging on a limb of a tree when I was along that road in 1938. It seems whoever did it, shot the horse behind the shoulder and then killed poor Ormes with either a stick or a rifle barrel.*

Australian folklore has had Coolon pinned as the murderer ever since, but an eyewitness report by an old man called 'T.C.W.' fifty years later clears his name.

Coolon (was) an outstanding bushman and a deadly rifle shot; he could hit anything as far as he could see. I knew Coolon very well, and he could be a good friend. I also knew Mrs Coolon, a fine Irishwoman, their eldest daughter Violet, and son Hector, the latter only a baby then. Regarding Constable Ormes's death on the Charters Towers-Clermont road, there was no foul play; he was not murdered nor was his horse shot.

I was coming into Clermont from the Suttor River about 1903, when, at the 60 Mile on the Charters Towers road, I found a dead man, perished from thirst, about three miles on the Clermont side of Lanark Station on Mistake Creek, then deserted. I pushed on to the Black Ridge Hotel. It was a gold mining place that was in full swing at the time, twelve miles from Clermont.

I reported finding the dead man to the police. Constable Ormes was sent out to bury the dead man. It was about three days to Christmas and very hot weather. So he rode out and stayed at the hotel that night and left next morning for the 60 Mile to bury the man. He said he could do it and be back that night, a round trip of 96 miles, no water anywhere, and only one horse to do the journey. He reached and buried the man and was no doubt trying to make the journey back in the night, was very thirsty and his horse galloped off the

> *road and ran into a fallen tree. This killed the horse, and the policeman was found dead some distance away from the horse; the limbs of the tree were responsible for his death also.*

Either way, Tom Coolon went about his business, kangaroo shooting in the Belyando River country, prospecting and working as a stockman. As one of his old comrades wrote:

> *(Tom) was also a marvellous bushman, and as a buckjump rider he was above average, although not in the Lance Skuthorpe class. Coolon was never guilty of riding a poor or weak horse, and if a buckjumper ran loose he would ride him, but not in a yard. He was one of the cleverest scrub riders that ever steered a horse through the mulga.*

Though he loved horses, Tom had a mortal fear of dogs, and would not suffer them anywhere near him. He would never refuse a bet, one night riding seven miles with no moon to locate a tomahawk he had left in the scrub, winning twenty pounds in the process. He also spent much more time away from his wife and children than near them. This last fact must have occurred to him, and he decided that it was time to settle.

One day, working around Yaccamunda Station, Tom came across a recently-pegged gold mine. The owner was nowhere to be seen. A few washes with the pan, however, told Tom that it was a rich claim, and he decided then and there that he wanted it.

The gold mine that Tom Coolon found on Yaccamunda Station was in a remote area, far from other diggings. With his knowledge of prospecting Tom suspected that it would be the start of something big. He cunningly learned everything he could about the man who had pegged the claim.

The words on a claim notice fixed to a stake meant nothing to the illiterate Tom. He instead used his tracking skills to learn of the claimant's movements. Footprints led to a nearby campsite, a small waterhole, and finally, horse tracks heading north towards Charters Towers.

Tom must have grinned to himself when he realised that the claimant was heading in the wrong direction. Mineral rights in this area, he knew, were under the jurisdiction of the mining warden in Clermont, to the south. Without wasting any time Tom saddled up and galloped off to find the warden, registering the claim in his own name. He was in full, legal possession of the claim when the man who originally pegged it, Luke Reynolds, arrived.

Reynolds had ridden all the way to Charters Towers, only to be told that he needed to go to Clermont, and was calling in to check on his claim on the way through. Tom was ready and waiting, his trusty lever-action Winchester close at hand.

'Who the bloody hell are you?' Reynolds asked.

'I'm the legal owner of this claim,' Tom replied. 'So if you value your life you'll turn around and keep riding.'

Reynolds was too smart to take Coolon head on, instead talking him into a partnership. This arrangement lasted only a few weeks before it fell apart. Reynolds decided that discretion was the better part of valour and pegged a new claim just along the ridge.

By this time Tom had built a sturdy hut and brought Catherine out to live with him. His mine had a thick seam of gold-bearing quartz, and hundreds of diggers flocked to the area, now named Mount Coolon. Within months the first stamper mill was on site, crushing piles of rich ore for the miners.

Finally, in his fifties, things seemed to have come together for Tom Coolon. He lived at home with Catherine. They had a garden and a flock of goats. The mine was making good money without too much hard work.

Yet, with no employees, Tom was obliged to travel away at times for supplies. Greedy eyes were watching when he rode off to Clermont with Catherine in late October, 1918. Under the law at the time a claim became void if it was left unattended by the owners.

A mining entrepreneur called Bernard Thompson waited until Coolon had been away for a few days then went to the local mining warden, filing for forfeiture of the mine because of Tom's absence. The warden backed him up, and Thompson now had title to the mine, obtained in a similar tricky way to how Tom had stolen the mine in the first place.

Thompson took on three partners to help work the claim: Harold Smith, Robert Wells and William Brown. When Tom returned from Clermont he found four armed strangers in legal possession of his mine. He flew into a terrible rage, demanding that the men leave immediately. They stood their ground. Thompson had decided to take Tom on in full knowledge of his reputation. He too was a hard man, and not easily cowed. Tom filed an appeal against the warden's decision but the District Court confirmed the forfeiture.

Tom was forced to watch from his hut as Thompson and Company brought gold ore up from the depths of a mine he had dug with his own hands.

On the morning of Wednesday November 13, 1918, Tom walked to the camp of a man called Charles Woodland, a JP, and asked him to take down his last will and testament. Once this was done, signed and witnessed, Tom walked back to his hut, fetching his Winchester and horse.

Riding up to his old claim he saw Bernard Thompson working up top. 'You've got five minutes to get off my claim,' Tom said.

Thompson shook his head. 'I'm not going.'

Tom raised the butt of his rifle to his shoulder and fired into the ground between them. Thompson went for the revolver on his belt. He fired but missed, and Tom's second shot took him under the arm, the third ploughed into his chest, killing him.

People had heard the shots, and news of Tom Coolon taking vengeance with a rifle spread like a grass fire. Men dived down mineshafts and hid. One of Tom's targets, Robert Wells, reckoned he owed his survival to sheer laziness, for he was having a smoke down the mine and couldn't be bothered going up when he heard someone yelling for him at the top.

The Native Bear Mine, Mount Coolon

Tom stopped at the Native Bear mine where he found an employee of Thompson's called William Bloom, who turned and ran. But to the old roo hunter a running man was easy prey. He brought him down with one shot.

Another man that Tom had intended to kill – Alexander Smith – fell to his knees and declared that he was Tom's friend, and that they had no quarrel. They shook hands and Tom declared that his plan was to kill a few more men and then 'do himself in.'

Tom rode fast, ahead of the rumours, to the stamp mill two miles away. There he found two more of Thompson's associates: Harold Smith and William Brown. He shot them both dead.

Finally, having killed four men, Tom rode off into the bush, leaving Catherine at home in the hut. Police from all over the district, led by an Inspector Quinn, scrambled to collect bodies and come to terms with what had happened.

A manhunt of epic proportions followed, but Tom, with his bush skills, had no trouble evading the police. Every man who had ever had reason to argue with Tom Coolon now believed himself a possible target. There was a sudden exodus from Mt Coolon and also Clermont of men who believed themselves to be on his hit list. On horseback and motor vehicle they fled, vowing to stay away until the murderer was caught.

Three days after the murders, Tom slipped through the police cordon and rode home to the hut he shared with Catherine. He kissed her for the last time, then turned the gun on himself. They found him there, in a pool of blood, with his wife of almost thirty years crying over him.

Mount Coolon in 1932 (John Oxley Library)

The Ragged Thirteen: 'Tea and Sugar' Bushrangers

Part legend, part fact, their adventures embellished and exaggerated around a thousand campfires, the story of the Ragged Thirteen has been beloved of bush story tellers for a hundred and thirty years.

The Ragged Thirteen were brilliant horsemen, fugitives, consummate bushmen, lovers of bush poetry and champions of the underdog. They embodied the new Australian nationalism of the latter part of the nineteenth century, with all its colour, larrikinism, love of the bush and suspicion of authority.

The story begins when a party of men travelling to the Hall's Creek goldfields via Queensland, led by Tom Nugent, joined up with another group heading for the same destination from South Australia and the Centre. The second group were led by a giant of a man, Alexander McDonald, better known as Sandy Myrtle. The two groups met up at Abraham's Billabong, on the Roper, just upstream from Mataranka's Bitter Springs, and the rum was soon flowing.

Tom Nugent took over as 'captain' of the gang, now

thirteen in number, and promised his new mates some serious mischief. From the Hunter Valley originally, Tom had moved to Queensland, working his way up to head stockman at Carandotta Station on the Georgina River. Later, cattle magnate John Costello hired Tom to manage Lake Nash Station on the Territory/Queensland border, but Tom always had a wild streak, and enjoyed life 'on the cross' more than working for a salary. He was, incidentally, good mates with Harry Readford, Australia's most famous cattle duffer.

Harry Readford (State Library of South Australia)

There are a many different perspectives on how the name 'Ragged Thirteen' came about. One story is that famous drover Nat Buchanan had seen the South Australian contingent camped at Johnston's Waterhole, further south, and called them a ragged bunch. Another contemporary credits a boundary rider named Steve Lacey with tagging them as 'The Thirteen.' Either way, the Ragged Thirteen they became, and they would soon be the most talked-about characters in the North.

Few accounts of their exploits agree on the names of those who made up the gang, but the most credible record, written by stockman Billy Linklater, records the names as Tom Nugent, Sandy Myrtle, Larrikin Bill Smith, Jim Fitzgerald, Bob Anderson, Hugh Campbell, Tommy the Rag, 'Wonoka' Jack and George Brown, 'New England' Jack Woods, Jim Carmody, Jack Dalley and Jimmy Woodford.

The Flora River in the 1880s

All were fine bushmen, with a passion for the outback. They looked down on members of the establishment, and most had Indigenous partners who rode with them on the journey west. A plant of at least forty good horses followed in their wake, controlled by young stock boys. The Ragged Thirteen loved good horses above all else.

The gang kicked off their exploits by walking from their campsite on the waterhole to the Abraham's Billabong store. Taking advantage of a 'new chum' storekeeper, they proceeded to ring up a fortune in worthless cheques, then made off with most of a beef carcass that was hanging on a gallows nearby.

When one of the store owners, renowned pugilist Matt Kirwan, arrived, he challenged the Thirteen to produce their best man to fight him. Hughie Campbell, a Scots seaman who had jumped ship in Port Augusta, volunteered, not only winning the fight, but breaking Kirwan's arm in the process. One observer claimed, however, that Kirwan was only just getting over a bout of malaria. 'Had he been in trim he would have whipped any one man in the bunch.'

Customs officer and policeman, Alfred Searcy relates in his book, By Flood and Field, that he and his partner, O'Donohue, first heard of the gang on the Roper.

When at the shanty at Abraham's Billabong, the keeper informed us that word had come from the Bar (Roper) that a gang of cowardly ruffians, known as 'The Ragged Thirteen,' were making their way to Kimberley 'on the nod,' that is, helping themselves to cattle from the stations, food from travellers and shanties, and using their revolvers when resisted. He greatly feared a visit, which he subsequently received, the scoundrels leaving him nothing but what he stood up in, and that, in the tropics, is precious little.

Searcy claims that he and his partner apprehended the gang, surprising them by offering tobacco, and then drawing their revolvers. The innovative lawmen apparently then cut their prisoners' braces so they were forced to hold up their trousers, making it hard for them to cause any trouble.

The timing of this coup, however, doesn't seem to fit with the facts. At best Searcy and O'Donohue held up only the Queensland crew, on their way west from Roper Bar. Either way, the gang members were soon released, for it turned out that there were no formal charges pending, on which they could be held.

Proceeding on their journey, the Thirteen robbed Jim Cashman's store in Katherine, then trekked down the Flora and Victoria Rivers to the huge Fisher and Lyon pastoral run, Victoria River Downs. Here, Tom Nugent posed as a land speculator to infiltrate the station, eating a slap-up dinner on the homestead verandah while the rest of the gang made off with several fine horses, and emptied the station store of horseshoes, nails, flour, tea and sugar.

Despite pursuit from the Territory police, the gang crossed the Negri River, into Western Australia, well provisioned and still ready for fun. They reached Hall's Creek when the gold rush was past its peak; but the town was still flourishing, with police, post office, numerous stores, hotels and grog shanties. Stories of gold nuggets lying around like chicken's eggs, were soon proved to be false.

Taking up a couple of claims, the Ragged Thirteen traded rifles for shovels and cradles. While digging for gold by day, however, the gang kept themselves afloat by duffing cattle from nearby stations at night; butchering them and selling the meat to hungry miners. 'New England' Jack Woods was the ringleader in these expeditions, and the nearby Durack cattle stations lost many a bullock to the Ragged Thirteen.

The gold mining itself, however, was proving to be much tougher than expected. It was certainly not as much fun as roving the country and skylarking. The gang's days were numbered, in any case. They were wanted in the Territory, and the WA 'traps' were also keen to pin horse-stealing charges on Tom. After six months or so of hard work and little return the gang dispersed.

Bob Anderson took up Tobermorey Station on the Eastern edge of the Territory, where he fathered a brace of children. A fall from a horse cut short his life. Sandy Myrtle returned to Central Australia where he set up a pub at the new Arltunga Goldfields. He reputedly grew so fat that he had to be lifted on and off his wagon by four strong assistants. Jimmy Woodford made a living finding and selling meteorites. George and Jack Brown worked as saw-millers before returning south. Hugh Campbell worked as a camp cook for a while, but grew ill and went home to Scotland to die. Jack Woods followed the goldfields, butchering other people's livestock wherever he went, and drinking the proceeds. The others spread out all over the north, including poor Jim Carmody, who drowned in the Katherine River while fishing.

Tom Nugent made a new home for himself on Banka Banka Station, near Tennant Creek, running the property successfully for many years, with a Garrwa (Borroloola) woman called Alice who became his life partner. He died in 1911, from dropsy, and his grave is still visible near the Telegraph Station today.

Alfred Searcy in bush gear.

The Eulo Queen

More than a century ago, when the town of Eulo was a thriving centre on the Western Queensland opal fields, one of Australia's most interesting women set out to make her mark. She was a short but striking redhead, spoke English, French and German, wore tight-fitting dresses over a voluptuous body, and had a fully-stocked bar in her bedroom.

Isobel Robinson, or the Eulo Queen, as she became known, was soon a legend from Quilpie to Lightning Ridge. Reputed to own the world's finest collection of opals, she was also one of country Queensland's biggest hoteliers, and boasted thousands of admirers. Every night she would hold court over the bar of the Royal Mail Hotel, carrying on with her delighted customers. Behind the fashionable gowns and diamond earrings, however, was a shrewd business brain.

Right from the beginning, Isobel had attitude. She was a crack rifle and pistol shot, a brilliant billiards player and apparently a shrewd card cheat. She also liked men, marrying three times. Her first husband died only a few weeks after the wedding. The second was a station manager called William Robinson who invited her out to the Paroo, and they leased their first hotel together in around 1886.

By 1902, when William died, they owned five pubs, a store and a butcher's shop, but trouble was on the way. The Licensing Commission decided that Isobel was not a fit person to hold a liquor licence. She countered this by bribing travellers camped along the river to act as proxies, but when they decided that this entitled them to free beer, the writing was on the wall.

The 'Eulo Queen' in her later years.

Isobel enjoyed several 'round the world' trips with rich squatters, then married again, to a man twenty-four years younger than her. The Eulo Queen's bad luck with husbands continued. He was killed in action during World War One.

Both the town of Eulo and its queen were in decline.

Alfred Bourke, writing in the Sydney Morning Herald in 1951, remembered meeting the Eulo Queen in his youth.

> *In 1921, I, a smooth-faced stripling, rode into Eulo with other drovers and met this still remarkable woman. Her 'domain' was then only a ramshackle store down by the banks of the Paroo. No trace of her beauty then remained, but her keen business instincts and feminine wiles were still much in evidence. Isobel died in a mental home in 1929, leaving an estate worth just thirty pounds.*

The Katherine Terrace Gunman

Monday, June 9 1952, and the outback town of Katherine was filled with station folk from hundreds of miles around, all in town for the race meeting that had been held over the weekend. An extravagant ball was planned for that night. By sunset, however, the town would be in a state of siege, doors barricaded shut, and armed men patrolling the streets.

In the late afternoon, a man in his twenties, Terrence Stapleton, approached taxi driver Leslie March, carrying a Lee Enfield .303 rifle. Turning the weapon on the driver, Stapleton forced him to drive around town aimlessly for half an hour.

'Shake hands with me, Les, as tomorrow you probably won't see me.'

'Why, are you going away?'

'No, but tonight blood will flow and I will go down in history. Now drop me at that cafe and don't wait around.' Stapleton then handed over a pocketful of loose change mixed with .303 cartridges.

Constable Condon had been sent in from his normal post at Maranboy (former tin mining town) to help keep order during the race meeting. He was in the dining room of the Commercial Hotel with his wife when he heard that an armed man was creating a disturbance.

The policeman walked outside and flagged down the same taxi driver who had just been menaced by the gunman, Leslie March, who carried him back along Katherine Terrace. Stapleton was by then standing outside the town's only cafe, brandishing his rifle and yelling.

Condon left the taxi and walked around the back, telling Stapleton to give up, but instead the gunman fired from the hip, hitting the policeman in the gut. Condon went down, but tried to get up. The Lee Enfield barked again and he fell in a heap.

Sergeant Joe Mannion arrived in the police truck and Stapleton opened fire, wounding Katherine's head cop in the thigh. Mannion tried to shoot back but his revolver got stuck in its holster. When he finally brought his weapon to bear, the gunman had run across the road and into the long grass. Constable Condon was by then lying dead on the road.

Stapleton disappeared into the scrub along the river, and word spread throughout the town that an armed murderer was at large. The ball was cancelled and no one left their homes without a weapon.

Stapleton was captured without further bloodshed the next day. He was tried three times due to appeals and a legal error, and was eventually found to have been legally insane while committing the crime. He was sent to Pentridge Prison in Victoria. Constable Condon was posthumously decorated for bravery and a Katherine Street still bears his name.

A comic that later appeared about the tragedy in a British crime magazine.

Nemarluk the Outlaw

Nemarluk was a fighting man of the Daly River people who would not be tamed. Born in 1911, by the 1930s he and a small band of young men were waging an effective guerrilla war against interlopers on his territory.

The Fitzmaurice and Daly River areas had never been settled. With the region's jagged sandstone gorges and winding rivers, pastoral pursuits were difficult, and supply routes subject to ambush. Nemarluk grew up in a time of conflict and, according to oral tradition, swore to keep his land free of outsiders, their laws, and their guns.

Three Japanese shark fishermen sailed their lugger into the Daly River near Port Keats. Their names were Nagata, Yoshida and Owashi. They anchored in a backwater and made contact with Nemarluk and his community, who were camped on the river bank.

Nemarluk was aware that the lugger was packed with stores, along with highly-prized iron and tobacco. He was also mindful of his oath to rid his lands of foreigners. He formulated a plan to attack and kill the Japanese without risking his people to their deadly guns.

The first step was to make the Japanese trust them. They

brought food aboard, served by the most attractive young women in the group. Nemarluk then suggested to Nagata, the captain, that he might go ashore to a lagoon and shoot as many ducks as he wanted.

Nagata took up the invitation, and was delighted to find that the lagoon really was alive with ducks. He shot a great number, walking further along the banks as he went. Waiting until the Japanese captain was thigh deep in water, Nemarluk gave the signal to attack.

After the murder, Nemarluk took the geese back to the lugger, telling the other Japanese that Nagata was attempting to shoot some kangaroos. Once they were aboard the Aborigines produced hidden weapons and killed the rest of the crew.

A frenzy of looting followed: more tobacco than they had seen in their lives, iron implements that could be filed down into spear points, along with blankets and vessels of all types. They also found guns.

It was rumours of guns in the possession of the group that provoked a strong reaction from the NT Police. Two parties were soon on the trail of Nemarluk and his comrades. The most feared of these was the mounted policeman Pryor, and the tracker, Bulbul.

Despite seeking refuge in the rugged Fitzmaurice region, most of Nemarluk's comrades were arrested for murder and faced the death sentence. Months later their leader was also captured.

Even then, Fannie Bay Jail could not hold this wild spirit. Nemarluk escaped by swimming across Darwin Harbour to the Cox Peninsula, a distance of at least eight kilometres.

Heading back into his homelands, Nemarluk continued to elude the police for years. This article from the Northern Standard newspaper gives an account of his capture.

> *Nemarluk was captured after two and a half years of continuous searching by officers and black trackers, who covered 21,000 miles of country. The capture occurred when Constable Birt was stationed at Timber Creek, in the western part of the Territory. Blacktrackers who were in his charge found Nemarluk at Legune Station in March, 1934. Constable Birt later escorted Nemarluk to Darwin to face a three-year-old charge of having been concerned in the murder of three Japanese at Port Keats.*
>
> *Nemarluk had been arrested after the murder, but escaped from the Fanny Bay Gaol, and was at large until Constable Birt's trackers found him. Bulbul, the leading tracker, was also responsible for the recapture of Minemara, another escaped native murderer who had been concerned in the killing of the Japanese, and who was captured in June last year.*

Nemarluk's exploits became the subject of a popular book by author Ion Idriess, who met the outlaw several times, and was impressed by his physical strength and demeanour.

The dust jacket introduced the book with the romantic assertion: 'Here now is Nemarluk's life story – the tragic adventures of the young chief who was a living Tarzan of the wilds.'

I doubt Idriess himself made that one up.

James 'Jimmy' Darcy

It had been a long day in the saddle for Walter and Thomas Darcy. They drew night watch duties, boxing the mob of cattle in on the river flats, while the rest of the crew slept. A rider came in from Wyndham with terrible news. Their brother Jimmy, also a stockman, had fallen from his horse on Ruby Plains Station and had been taken to Hall's Creek on a cart with severe internal injuries.

The brothers wasted no time in going to Jimmy's aid. Making sure the cattle were in safe hands they mounted fresh horses and rode for 140 miles before stopping at Turkey Creek for remounts. By the time they reached Hall's Creek they had covered 250 miles without rest. The last 110 miles they smashed in just 15 hours.

Finally, arriving at Hall's Creek, they found that there being no hospital, Jimmy was in the care of the Postmaster, Fred Tuckett. After a visit with their brother the boys were troubled. Jimmy's lower abdomen was swollen and red, and he was barely conscious. There was no doctor for a thousand miles and the situation seemed hopeless.

'He looks like he's dying Mister,' they pleaded with the postmaster, 'you have to save him …'

'I've sent a telegram to Perth. They'll send someone on the steamer.'

The brothers groaned. 'That'll be weeks. Jimmy could die by then. He needs surgery.'

Another telegram was sent to Perth. This time to a man who had instructed Fred in first aid a few years earlier. Was it possible that a surgeon in Perth could help with the patient via telegram? This novel idea bore fruit, and a back-and-forth diagnosis of a ruptured bladder, complicated by infection, was made. The pressure had to be released, and only Fred could do the job!

Fred Tuckett

While the brothers waited anxiously outside, the postmaster made an incision with a razor blade, then painstakingly stitched the wound back up, with a drain in place. The rudimentary operation helped at first, but over the following days there was little improvement. The Perth surgeon decided, via telegram, that a major operation was needed.

By this time major newspapers across the country were reporting the story, and a Dr Holland was making his way up the vast Western Australian coast by boat, still much too far away for the operation to wait.

Again Mr Tuckett sterilised his razor, and with the wires running hot, completed a difficult operation that was basically successful. Australians all across the country, welcome for the respite from war news, breathed a sigh of relief.

It would have been nice if Jimmy made a full recovery, but unfortunately his condition was complicated by the malaria he had been suffering from for months. Again he deteriorated until his life hung by a thread.

Yet Dr Holland had by then arrived in Derby, and a team of bushmen were standing by with a Model T Ford to carry him to Halls Creek.

Walter and Thomas Darcy urged their desperately ill brother to hold on, that help was on the way. But the wild Kimberley was not kind to motor vehicles. The Model T limped slowly closer, plagued by engine trouble and flat tyres.

Jimmy Darcy died the day before the Perth surgeon arrived. His grieving brothers laid him to rest in the Hall's Creek cemetery.

The events of those weeks affected Holland so deeply that he became a founding member of the Royal Flying Doctor Service, which would go on to save thousands of lives, many with similar injuries to Jimmy Darcy.

The Tragedy of Joe Flick

When Joe Flick barricaded himself in a galvanised iron hut at Lawn Hill Station in 1889, then shot a police constable in the heart, killing him instantly, he was touted in the newspapers of the day as murderous. But what was the history behind those three terrible days when Joe killed two men, and wounded another?

Joe was born in around 1867, in New South Wales. His father was a German-born stockman called Henry Flick, and his mother a traditional Kamilaroi woman. It's likely that she was abducted by force, and she soon bore him a son, Joe. For part of Joe's childhood he was looked after by police families while Henry was in prison for the violent kidnap of another Indigenous woman.

Working as a stockman, drifting northwards through Queensland, Henry ended up on Lawn Hill Station, at first as a stockman, then as a miner in Frank Hann's fledgling silver mining enterprise. Young Joe grew up on horseback, learning his formidable bush skills along the Gregory River, and Lawn Hill Creek.

As a young man Joe had the reputation for being quietly spoken, avoiding alcohol and tobacco. He was also regarded as a superb horseman.

The Police Quarters, Normanton (NLA)

In early 1888 he had a bitter dispute with the owner of the nearby Brook Hotel, Jim Cashman. Most reports suggest that the problem occurred over Joe's interest in a housemaid at the hotel. Other contemporaries relate that Joe's mother, or at least his father's current woman, was assaulted by a male employee of the hotel and Joe confronted the owner.

Whatever the reason, Joe drew his revolver and fired a shot at Cashman, narrowly missing the hotelier's wife, a former house maid herself. This wild act set Joe on a collision course with police, and he was soon convinced to give himself up. After his arrest, Joe was chained and taken to Normanton lock up, though he soon escaped. With the police in close pursuit he ran for the Territory border. There, in the upper Nicholson, he was speared in the leg by Waanyi tribesmen, who were fighting a frontier war against the pastoralists and drovers. Joe, being on horseback and dressed as a white man, was a target.

After a few weeks of recuperation, healing at a cattle camp on Cresswell Creek, Joe rode to Hodgson Downs Station, on a tributary of the Roper. There he became one of the best stockman that the manager, Crawford by name, had seen, and he might have stayed there indefinitely as a peaceable, hard-working ringer.

The Roper Police, however, were tipped off that Flick was nearby. Troopers Stott and Haedge arrested Joe, and prepared to ride with him for Palmerston, as Darwin was called in those days.

Travelling along the Roper, they camped near McMinn's

Bluff, and there Joe made a run for the bush. Chained as he was, including a neck-ring fasted with a Yale lock, his progress was slow. Stott and his trackers came up to Joe in thick scrub that evening. A warning shot rang out, then another aimed at Joe. He fell to the ground, wounded in the back.

What followed is a sad indictment of the justice system of the day. Only half healed, Joe rotted in Fannie Bay Gaol, while Palmerston's Chief Justice Pater all but begged the Queensland Police to come and get their prisoner. Sixteen times over four months, Joe was forced to front court, only to be remanded in custody again.

When a Queensland policeman, Harry Hasenkamp by name, finally arrived, he failed to bring the correct extradition warrant, and the exasperated Pater released Joe. He was, unfortunately immediately rearrested, and charged with a different offence, one that was covered by the warrant. Joe was taken by steamer to Normanton, via Thursday Island.

Back in the Normanton lockup, it seems incredible that Joe could have escaped again, yet he used a small saw, smuggled in by sympathisers, to remove sections of the floorboards. Despite his cell-mate turning informer, Joe was soon on the run again. After a few weeks in the upper Gregory, he arrived at Turn-off Lagoon, where pub owner Mary Theresa Anderson reported his presence after her gardener spotted Joe 'lurking' around the house.

Locating the police horse paddock, Joe took the ones he wanted, then mustered the others onto the road, drove them two miles out of town and shot them. It was at this point that the Queensland police realised that they had a dangerous man on the loose. The idea that they had created this escalation, partly through their own actions, must not have occurred to them.

Senior Constable Alfred Wavell, originally from the Isle of Wight, took up the challenge of bringing Joe in. Alfred made his last Will and Testament, collected his tracker, Garrie, and set off in pursuit. At Bannockburn he found a wide-awake resident who complained of Joe riding up in the middle of the night and throwing rocks at his roof.

Soon after Alfred met up with a comrade, Constable

Gunn, who gave him a second tracker, Trooper Noble.

On Joe's trail, in the headwaters of Widdallion Creek on Lawn Hill country, they came upon the fugitive, who abandoned his packhorse and made a run for it. The police gave chase, but lost Joe in the wild country to the south.

The next morning, while Wavell and his men breakfasted in the dining hall at Lawn Hill Creek, Joe was seen trying to catch a new mount in the house paddock there. The police galloped down to confront him, firing wildly, managing a lucky shot that took Joe's horse out from under him.

Lawn Hill Station (Queensland State Library)

Running to the station itself, Joe holed up in the old dining room, now quarters for the head stockman, where he found a 'choke bore shotgun' and a revolver along with hundreds of cartridges. He opened the shutter and prepared to defend himself.

Constable Alfred Wavell made the mistake of trying to parley with Joe, and received a fatal wound in the chest when he stepped from the cover of the station store. Frank Hann, the station owner, tried the same tactic and was badly, though not mortally wounded.

A build-up season storm set in, during which the two leaderless troopers, and a neighbour, Fred Doyle, desperately tried to hold Joe in the room until reinforcements arrived. In the meantime they fired repeatedly into the hut, and Joe was struck in the ankle and stomach.

Despite these wounds, he slipped out that night, down

the steep escarpment that led to the creek. There he took up position between two huge paperbark trees, where he waited for the police party to come after him. He watched, the next morning, as they followed his blood trail down the cliff. Their numbers had swelled with a couple of stockmen, Harry Shadforth and Dan Carlyon, who had arrived to help. Frank Hann had also shown his legendary toughness by rising from his bed to exact revenge.

Joe's first shot from cover killed Nym, one of Frank Hann's Waanyi servants. The rest of the party took cover. A long stalemate ensued. Through the afternoon they fired hundreds of rounds into Joe's hiding place, and even set fire to the grass in an attempt to burn him out.

That night, Joe Flick, struck by at least nine bullets, passed away. He was buried upside down, facing hell, in an unmarked grave next to the white man he had killed, Alfred Wavell. Nym was buried some eighty metres away.

Captain Moonlite

The Capture of Moonlite (Victorian State Library)

It was Saturday, November 15, 1879, and the McDonald family, at Wantabadgery Station, half way between Wagga Wagga and Gundagai, were settling down for the evening. A shepherd galloped in from further down the Murrumbidgee with the news.

"I seen a gang of horsemen coming up along the river," he said breathlessly. "I swear it's Captain Moonlite and his men."

While family and employees alike took refuge inside the house, seven horsemen rode out of the night. A pounding on the door followed. Claude McDonald, the station owner, opened the door a crack, revealing Captain Moonlite himself, dressed in a dark cloak, as dashing as his reputation.

"Good evening," the bushranger said in his cultured Irish accent. "My men and I are starving. Can we trouble you for bread and tea?"

"Ride off, and don't come back," came the answer. Furious, Moonlight stalked back to his men and horses. The gang members loaded their revolvers and Snider rifles. Gunfire was exchanged, and within a few minutes, Moonlite had taken control of the homestead. The gang rounded up the neighbours, twenty-five in all, and raided the Australian Arms Hotel, a mile or two down the Gundagai Road, taking all the liquor they could carry.

Moonlite and his men ate and drank into the night. To entertain themselves they forced young women to play the piano or sing, and held a mock trial of a man who tried to escape. One brave stockman attempted to charge the guns, but was knocked down and restrained.

Four troopers, arriving on the scene, had little chance of taking down the well-armed gang, who fired at them through the windows. Riding off for reinforcements, however, the troopers were soon back with five more men from Wagga Wagga. The policemen surrounded the homestead, and the Moonlite gang, seeing the odds against them, slipped out by a side door.

Fighting a rear-guard action, firing from outbuildings and neighbouring farms, Moonlite and his men finally found themselves penned in to an outdoor kitchen. Gus Wreneckie, just fifteen years old and by far the youngest member of the gang, was shot and killed. There was no turning back now. A bullet from Moonlite struck home, killing Constable Edward Webb-Bowen.

Captain Moonlite's right-hand-man, James Nesbitt fell also, shot dead, and this was a bitter moment for Moonlite. He fell to his knees, cradling his dying mate in his arms. Constable McGlede saw his opportunity, charging the kitchen, disarming the leader and scattering the gang. It was all over.

Only Moonlite himself, and a man called Tom Rogan,

felt the hangman's noose, the other three survivors were given long prison sentences. The legend that grew up around Moonlite's life kept the public interested for years, and the facts slowly faded from memory.

Captain Moonlite, whose real name was Andrew George Scott, was surely Australia's strangest bushranger. The Irish-born engineer, soldier and lay-preacher, though violent at times, was more of a talker than a fighter, and had an inflated opinion of his own worth. He had a history of swindling friends and opportunistic robbery. The cape was just part of his penchant for dressing up.

His first major heist involved robbing gold bullion from one of his best friends, then leaving a note claiming the robbery in the name of 'Captain Moonlite.' He later caused a mass break out at Ballarat gaol by tunnelling through a wall and into neighbouring cells. After years of trouble with the law, and a second stint in prison, he formed a gang with six other slum dwellers and ex-cons and headed for the bush.

The police and public took Moonlite seriously, but other bushrangers and the hard men of Australia's countryside did not. Legend has it that when operating in Northern Victoria, Moonlite sent a message to Ned Kelly and his gang, suggesting that they join forces. The answer apparently came back from Ned that if Moonlite or his men came anywhere near him he'd shoot them down like dogs.

Much has been made of Scott's relationship with Nesbitt. There's no doubt that they were unusually close. Was Captain Moonlite, with his love of the theatrical, and deep feelings for his friend Nesbitt, Australia's only gay bushranger? We'll never know for sure, but we do know that Nesbitt's death broke his heart.

"My dying wish is to be buried beside my beloved James Nesbitt," Scott wrote before his hanging, "… the man with whom I was united by every tie which could bind human friendship. We were one in hopes, in heart and soul and this unity lasted until he died in my arms."

Note: A plaque commemorating the Siege of Wantabadgery hangs on the wall of Gundagai's Criterion Hotel.

SETTLERS AND PIONEERS

The JC

In the late 1860s pastoralist and adventurer John Costello rode west from his holdings on Kyabra Creek, exploring the Channel Country out to the Diamantina. One night he camped beside a small creek, where he stripped back the bark of a bauhinia tree and carved his initials, JC.

That tree became a popular stopping place for travellers, and when an enterprising hotelier built a mud-brick pub on the site, he called it the JC Hotel. The government surveyor was sent in to lay out a town, but he refused to call the new town JC because it wasn't proper. He named the place Canterbury instead, but to locals the name never changed.

In the mid-1880s the pub was being run by two

men in partnership: Manners and Dalton. Not only did they spruce the place up, but apparently Mrs Dalton was a popular figure behind the bar. A visitor in 1885 reported that nearly thirty men sat down to eat breakfast at the hotel.

The owner of nearby Waverney Station, a man by the name of Gibbs, built a store next to the pub. It was apparently "fully stocked with all the requirements of a country store." A post office was opened in 1891, and ran for a couple of years before being downgraded to a receiving office.

In 1893 the pub was being run by George and Elizabeth Geiger. Their son, also named George, not quite two and a half, was playing in the yard when he wandered off. One story goes that he had a pet lamb, and when it was taken by a dingo, he followed.

Every available adult, including some capable trackers, were enlisted to find young George, but the flock of goats kept by the family had obliterated his tracks, and the mulga scrub made it hard to see more than a few yards. They found him in the end, much too late, and the dingos had finished him off. His grave still stands in the small cemetery there.

The pub was the venue for regular dances, and an annual race meeting. Most importantly it gave travellers a friendly place to stop between Windorah and Bedourie. The beer flowed for another half century before the manager of Waverney bought it for a pittance and shut it down. He was sick of his stockmen spending their free time there and riding home drunk.

Augusta Marion Gaunt

Long before drover Charlie Gaunt rode the plains of Western Queensland and the Gulf Track across to the Kimberleys with the Duracks, his mother was a passenger on an immigrant ship, plying the seas from England to a new life in Australia.

The family sailed on the Royal Mail Steamship *Africa*, in late 1852, and for five months nine-year-old Augusta Marion Fuller made her family's thinly partitioned space on the steerage deck her home. 450 immigrants were sandwiched into this converted cargo hold at the stern, with enough head space only for children to stand. The sun barely penetrated, and the air stank of close-packed, unwashed humanity.

Hundreds of people used two overflowing privies with queues all day and night, talking or arguing in Scottish, Irish, Welsh, and every dialect of England. All were desperate poor. The dangers and possibilities ahead were the main topics of conversation.

Augusta's father, Adam Fuller, was a sick man. He needed a warm place to live. He was also a bankrupt. Augusta didn't really know what it meant except that it had happened to him twice and that they had no money. She understood that Australia was their last chance for happiness.

All the time, day in, day out, the side-paddle churned and the *Africa* faced the big green ocean swells. Augusta sang nursery rhymes to the rhythms of the steam engines.

Augusta's mother, Anna, held the tiny hands of her daughters. 'The Mate told me that we'll reach Melbourne in just one more day,' she said. 'Your uncle George will be there to meet us. He'll help us. Da will get well then. God won't let him die.'

From then on they counted the hours and the miles, while Adam held on, falling lower and lower. He was still breathing, however, when the ship passed through Port Phillip heads and the *Africa* came alongside the Town Pier in Hobson's Bay.

Augusta looked out from the rail, to another long pier that jutted into the bay to the north. There were building frames visible behind the beach near the Customs House. Further on was the vast slum of Canvas Town, a city of tents, the home of thousands of hopefuls on their way to and from the Goldfields.

Augusta had never seen her Uncle George but she scanned the crowd as they waited out on the concourse with their bags. Slowly the arrivals wandered off to their relatives or prepared to cross the sandy track to the settlement of Melbourne on the Yarra, on foot or by one of the many horse drawn vehicles for hire.

The unloading of the ships' cargo started. Corpses were carried out first. One in twenty of those who had set out from Liverpool had already been buried at sea along the way.

Augusta and her family were spared the tragedy of death by only one day. The following afternoon, Adam Fuller died, and they had no choice but to move into the Houseless Immigrants home.

Anna sent a desperate message to her brother George, who was supposed to have met them when they arrived. The following advertisement appeared in the Melbourne Argus on Saturday April 23, 1853.

GEORGE JOHNSON – Your sister MRS MARIA FULLER is very desirous of seeing you. Apply to Mr Barry,

Storekeeper Flinders Lane, West.

That night when the destitute little family returned to their room, a big, sunburned man in his mid-twenties was waiting for them. Augusta watched as her mother ran into his arms. He was rugged looking and a little scary.

The man finally left Anna's embrace, and looked down at the girls.

'Hullo,' he said. 'I'm your Uncle George.'

He smelled of whisky. Augusta hid behind Amelia's legs.

> GEORGE JOHNSON—Your Sister, Mrs. MARIA FULLER, who arrived here per ship Africa, is very desirous of seeing you Apply to Mr. Barry, Storekeeper, Flinders-lane, West. 36843

George was living in Ballarat, where the gold boom was in full cry. Augusta's mother Anna was nothing if not resilient, and after a few years of living on the charity of her brother, she fell in love again. Henry William Cooper was the son of a coach builder from Dublin and owner of the Burrumbeet Hotel, on the shores of Lake Burrumbeet, near Ballarat.

Anna lied about her age to the celebrant, and most likely to her new husband as well. She was forty three years old by then, but the marriage certificate lists her age as just thirty-five. Partly, perhaps, for the vanity of her husband, who was thirty-seven at the time.

Augusta was twelve years old by then, almost certainly a flower girl. The ceremony took place on the north shore of Lake Burrumbeet, perhaps on one of those perfect spring days that Ballarat can produce when it feels like showing off.

George was there to give Anna away, and no doubt he did his best to drink the hotel dry at the reception afterwards. (The newspapers of the day were sprinkled with George's minor run-ins with the law, mainly for drunk and disorderly behaviour and the odd fight.)

The wedding was a triumph, certainly much better than Anna's taste in men deserved.

Within twelve months, however, Henry William Cooper was insolvent, and the Burrumbeet Hotel was sold for less than half of what he paid for it. In fact, a meeting of creditors was informed that Henry had paid three times the true value of the hotel in the first place.

Augusta and her sisters were again forced onto the charity of their family.

Catherine Coleman – Pioneer

Catherine Cecilia Coleman wasn't famous, but was typical of a generation of Australian settlers. She was born in Maitland, NSW in 1856, eldest of ten children. She married in 1871, at the age of 15, and had the first of her own children a couple of years later.

Her husband, John Douglas Coleman, was determined to make his mark in business, and in 1887 the young family packed up and moved north. Their new home would be the land of opportunity, Western Queensland, a wilderness only just then being opened up to cattle and sheep.

Arriving at Whittown (Isisford), near Longreach, the Barcoo River had broken its banks and was in full flood. Catherine's quick-thinking brother Dan placed the young Catherine and her children in a large draper's packing case and towed them across on a rope.

John moved them further west to the fledgling town of Forest Grove (Arrilalah), a natural stop for drovers and teamsters making their way up the Thomson River.

At Forest Grove John and Catherine built the mud-brick Club Hotel and a store, operating both for many years with the help of the resourceful Dan. The babies kept coming, and Catherine gave birth to ten children overall while mobs of cattle and sheep came up along the river bed, and dusty men in felt hats rode in to slake their thirst. Picnic races, held every few months, brought a colourful crowd of riders, punters and revellers in from stations and nearby towns.

Billiard Saloon and chemist at Forest Grove (QLD State Library).

Then, in September 1888, the dream ended. John fell ill, and did not recover. He died on the 26th of September, and was buried up behind the pub.

Catherine sold up and moved to Isisford, where she lived for 66 years. Her brother Dan also remained in the district. Even in her eighties Catherine was still slim and active, and could apparently read without glasses. Catherine died in August 1944 at the age of 88. Only four of her ten children outlived her. At the time of her death she was survived by 30 grandchildren, 29 great grandchildren, and 12 great-great grandchildren. Most still lived in the Isisford district at that stage.

There is nothing left of the once thriving town of Arrilalah now but ruins, some signage placed by the

Longreach Historical Society, and one gravestone.

The 'Petticoat' Drovers

Esther Jenkins was born at Gingie Station, near Walgett, NSW, in 1879. She was one of seven children. The family were dirt-poor, mostly barefoot and living in hand-me-downs. The Jenkins clan had, at that stage, already been in Australia for almost a century.

When Esther was nine years old the family pulled up stumps, stacked everything in a dray, and shifted to Northwestern Queensland, making a home in Barclay Street, Camooweal. Esther's father worked as a carrier, carting stores for outlying stations, and bringing goods down from the busy port at Burketown.

Esther was a robust kid, red haired and freckled. She stood up for herself in that outback town, rarely backing down to bullies of either gender. But despite the Jenkins family's fighting spirit, that remote town was a hard place to live in those days.

When Esther was ten years old her brother Thomas died of malaria and dysentery in Hughenden hospital. He was just twenty-four years old. Medical treatment was widely spaced and often basic. The lack of medicines and the necessity of long travel times to reach help meant that even minor injuries could turn septic and lead to death.

As she grew, Esther became a talented runner, winning races across Western Queensland, and becoming well known across the state.

Yet, for all her talent, Esther's childhood was soon over. She was just fourteen years old when she married James Bennett in 1894. The pair tied the knot in Camooweal and had two sons, Jim and George Bennett.

The marriage did not last. In 1902 Esther met and married John Bohning. John was born Johann Böhning in Hamburg, Germany, in 1878, but anglicised his name.

By 1904 John was at Rocklands Station, building earthen water tanks. He was a hard worker, undertaking punishing physical labour in one of the most extreme climate zones on earth. Yard building was one of his specialities, with the small but tough Esther working as hard as he did.

Elsie Bohning age 15 years AIM Collection

Meanwhile, Esther gave birth to the first of their children. By the time Elsie was born, in Borroloola in 1909, John was, like his father in law, in business for himself as a carrier, running a dray from Camooweal across the Barkly Tablelands to the Territory stations, usually with his family in tow.

It was a harsh life with young children, and when Elsie's older sister Ellen fell sick on the trail they returned to Camooweal. It was too late to save her, however, and she was thirteen when they lost her. Another daughter, Helen, died near the Queensland/NT border and was buried alongside the track.

Elsie on a Donkey (NT Times)

War with Germany broke out in 1914, and with posters of blood-stained 'Huns' on shopfronts and street corners, anti-German feeling was on the rise. German nationals were being interred in southern states and it must have seemed that the safest bet for John Bohning was to get as far 'outback' as possible, at least while the war lasted.

In 1917 Esther's father William died of 'senility' and an ulcerated foot that turned gangrenous, in the Camooweal Cottage Hospital. This was, to Esther, the signal for a change in her family's circumstances.

Tired of the nomadic life, she now demanded that the family settle somewhere permanently. They looked for property around Renner Springs, near the Overland Telegraph Line, in the NT. A parcel of land became available to the south — twelve hundred square miles in area, one hundred and fifty kilometres north of where Tennant Creek is now. They named this new station Helen Springs, after one of their dead girls.

In those early days, the family lived in a hut, with a lean-to kitchen. But Esther was an inventive cook and able to improvise almost anything; turning her hand to preserves, leather tanning, even boot making. With only one trip to 'town' every six months, making essentials from local materials was an important part of station life.

Esther's daughter Elsie, it turned out, had a talent too. Writing. At the age of thirteen, in 1922, she penned the first of many letters to the Northern Territory Times. Her pen name was 'The Little Bush Maid,' and her precociousness and sincerity won her a wide audience.

> *We rise at break of day. Jack with bridle over his arm is streaking around the home paddock, after the working horses; Edith and self are making for the cow yard, armed with buckets and billycans for the milking. Alick and Bill are racing for the goat yard, Alick with a kerosene tin nearly as big as himself. Bill has two billycans. Mum is preparing breakfast and putting the separator together. Dad is churning the butter. He has an old demijohn with the top cut off it for a churn. It's a very good churn. It keeps the cream sweeter and cooler than tin ware. He has a bit of board for a bat; a little short bat with a long handle on it. He stirs the cream around and around until it breaks into little lumps. Then he pours cold water out of a water bag into it. This is for extracting the butter milk, otherwise butter will not keep.*

Growing up on the station, far from any school and long before the coming of School of the Air, Elsie was taught by her dad, and loved describing station life to her (mainly Darwin based) audience of readers.

'What have you got for breakfast, mum?'

'Bacon and eggs; they are in the stove keeping warm. Fresh butter, gooseberry and rosella jam, tomato sauce, ripe gooseberry, cream and tomatoes, all grown on the farm and butter-milk scones. What more do you want?

'I want some golden syrup; bread and butter is no good without treacle on top to sweeten it'.

'You had better run to the store and get a tin, then; this one is empty.'

Breakfast is over. Edith takes over the kitchen to cook the dinner. Edith is a good cook. Jack and Dad are erecting some wooden troughing for watering stock. They went out into the scrub and cut big forest giant and old man gum trees; all hollowed out by white ants. Then they cut them into the shape of a trough and place one end inside the other; then tack tin over the point, and choke up any leak with fat and ashes. Mum is the fat and ashes carpenter. Alick and Bill are pumping away at another well with their donkey. They are pumping into the creek and garden and they are keeping me busy, opening and closing drains for the vegetable patch. The boys fork the well, then put the donkey in the paddock and let the

> *well make up again. After lunch they pump again. Then I make for Shingle Hut and tidy up a bit and give the boys a lesson.*

Every year the family mustered their fat bullocks and drove them to the railhead, at Oodnadatta, South Australia. Elsie first took her place on that trip in 1924, at the age of fifteen, cheered on by her friends at the Northern Territory Times.

> *That wonderful little woman, Miss Elsie Bohning of Helen Springs Station on the edge of the Barclay Tablelands, is on the road with a mob of cattle making for Oodnadatta, thence by rail to Adelaide. The distance to be travelled by road is over 700 miles, and some of the stages are long and dry. Miss Bohning is an exceptionally good hand among cattle, and is probably the best hand in the droving camp. We sincerely hope that our gallant little friend (who, by the way, writes us an interesting letter occasionally) will come through this prodigious and very trying journey with safety and profit to herself and family.*

The Southern press, always keen on an outback human interest story, waded in, and before long Esther, Edith and Elsie were known as the 'petticoat drovers'. This didn't stop their status as drovers being challenged by males, however, particularly when they were forced to travel without John.

The rest of the time, station life went on – visitors were rare but always good for some invented entertainment. Impromptu horse races were a favourite diversion.

> *A horse race out on the old cattle camp is a matter of absorbing interest and in a country where children learn to ride when they are three, there is not much*

> *that grown up men have left to learn about horses. After the midday meal was over, Jack ran up the paddock horses and we had no less than five races. My luck was in. I had two wins on Old Jack. We nicknamed him Boomerang Jack because when he was a frisky young foal running by his mother's side another horse kicked (him) and broke his leg below his hock. Mum put his leg in splints and bandaged it up, but the young scamp got his bandages off before his leg was properly knitted, with the result that it is a little crooked. His leg is quite strong; he can wheel the flying scrubbers and draft on the cattle camp and win races at a picnic.*

Elsie loved her pets, and these changed regularly. There were goats of course. On almost all stations of the day the goat herd supplied milk, along with tasty meat – a welcome alternative to beef – and the small carcasses could be eaten quickly before starting to spoil. An Aboriginal woman or teenager was often employed to herd them.

At one stage Elsie had a baby echidna, (or porcupine as she called it) and a lizard she referred to as a 'mountain devil' that fed exclusively on ants.

Remote living had its pitfalls, and in 1925 Elsie was working in the yards when she was charged by a bullock. The Bohning kids were adept at yard work and she clambered up the rails at speed, unfortunately losing her balance at the top and falling down the other side. A dislocated shoulder was the result.

The nearest medical facility was at Maranboy, hundreds of miles away, and it was a long trip by wagon. But the dislocated shoulder was soon clicked back into place under anaesthetic.

As Elsie grew to young adulthood, the station became more liveable. In 1927 the old lean-to kitchen was finally replaced with a 'real' kitchen.

> *The boys completed our new kitchen yesterday and I am shifting camp tomorrow; so will be able to have things very 'stylish' on Helen Springs then, and the opening ceremony will be held on June 9th; so all friends come along and hear our little jazz band. It consists of a comb; leaf; mouth organ and kerosene tins and we have an excellent sand and tar floor on which dancing may be indulged. At 10 pm we will have coffee, tea, cocoa, jam tarts, honey roll, cream puffs and cucumber and tomato sandwiches. So bidding you all a hearty welcome I conclude. Au revoir until Saturday night.*

In 1930 a drover taking cattle to his holdings south of Tennant Creek stopped at Helen Springs on his way through. Frederick Harris was fifteen years older than Elsie, but he was the kind of man she admired, and at twenty-one years she was ready to leave the family station.

Frederick was thirty-seven years of age and had cut his teeth working as a stockman and drover in Western Australia. Now the owner of McLaren Valley Station he must have been unable to believe his luck to win Elsie's heart. She was lively, intelligent, as good in the cattle yards or range as any man, and knew how to run a station. She had also inherited the blonde good looks of her German father.

Elsie was furious when the Northern Standard newspaper reported her engagement to Frederick Arthur Harris. She criticised their report in a letter to the Times.

> *I notice the 'Standard' had already announced any engagement. It seemed rather presumptuous on their part, as no such information had been forwarded, to them from any of the par-*

> ties concerned. I am anxious to know why they call my fiancé, a 'new comer' as he has been in the country for the last four years at least. I will be obliged if the 'Standard' will kindly leave me out of their paper until they have personal authority from myself or some other member of the family to print such information.'

The Standard responded with the following.

> Sometime ago we published the engagement of Miss E. Bohning, and for this we are the subject of a paragraph in the last issue of our contemporary, headed, 'A note of Reproof from Miss E Bohning.' The young lady in question indirectly admits her engagement but appears to be annoyed because the Standard beat her to it. As the 'Little Bush Maid' Miss Bohning has contributed letters to the Times for years, apparently loving the limelight, she wants a monopoly of the news. As far as Miss Bohning being obliged if the 'Standard' will 'leave me out of their paper until they have authority from myself ...' we desire to tell Miss Bohning that the Standard is being run as a newspaper and if we receive authentic news of sufficient importance to warrant publication we will print it whether it meets with the wishes of Miss Bohning or otherwise.

The wedding was held at Helen Springs, with a guest list that included most of the big pastoral families of the times. Everything from dresses to the cake itself were ordered months earlier and delivered through the somewhat irregular mail service.

Looking charming in an instep length flared skirt of heavyweight crepe-dechene, with, flared sleeves, white tulle veil, and carrying a wreath of orange blossoms, Elsie, youngest daughter of Mr and Mrs John Bohning, of Helen Springs, was wedded to Mr Frederick Harris, of McLaren Valley Station, Central Australia, by the Rev H. Griffiths, of Katherine, at the residence of the bride's parents, at 3 pm on Wednesday, October 5th, the bride being given away by her father. The bride also carried a sheath of white oleanders cut from the garden of her parents. Miss Betty Litchfield of Darwin, was bridesmaid and chose a frock of ankle length rose pink silk- georgette with pleated sleeves. She wore a posy of pink oleanders and carried a bouquet of orange blossoms. Mr Mick Bohning, brother of the bride, was best man. The bride's gift to the groom was a traveller's set, the groom's gift to the bride being an engraved dressing table set. The gift to the bridesmaid was a string of pearls, which was worn at the wedding, and that to the best man a pair of hair brushes in a leather case.

The two-tier wedding cake, which was the work of Balfour's, Adelaide, was beautifully iced, and decorated. Amongst those present were Misses May, Josephine, and Eileen O'Shea (of Katherine), Mrs H. Griffiths, (Katherine) Mr J. Sargeant (Newcastle Waters) Mr B. Kirby (Birdum), Mr R. Reid (Newcastle Waters), Mr S. Y. C. Smith (Newcastle Waters), Mr G. Fraser (Barrow

Creek), Mr J. Althaus (Nutwood Downs Station), Mr C. Burkitt (Newcastle Waters Station) Mr J. Bennett (Delamere Station), Mr B. Litchfield .(Darwin), Mr C. Berg (Newcastle Waters), Mr G. Nicholls (Newcastle Waters), Mr E. Martin (Powells Creek), Mr D. Cowper (Helen Springs) and Mr B. Bohning (Helen Springs).

Elsie Bohning was living in a time of rapid change. During her time at Helen Springs, then McLaren Creek Station, she saw the changeover from camels, bullocks and packhorses as the main means of transport, to cars, trucks and aeroplanes.

Today should be a red letter day for the waybacks. A new era is dawning; motor transport for the N.T. The first load (of cattle) per motor lorry was delivered at Powell's Creek from the railhead at Oodnadatta in S.A., a distance of 700 miles. The driver Mr W McKay in-formed me that the trip was accomplished in 8 days and they came in easy stages, they did not go in for record breaking stunts, the only place they had a bit of trouble was at the McLaren. I remember this creek – a nasty, heavy sandy uphill pull on the north bank, but on the south bank going towards Alice Springs it is hard. The McLaren is about 6 miles north of Bonnie Well. Mr McKay was accompanied by the Fizzer, the Fizzer knows every inch of the road from Powell's Creek to the Alice having ridden that mail for about 8 years. The driver informs me that the road will be quite alright for motor transport if a little is done to the roads. I am tip-

ping that camels, our ships of the desert, will in about 10 years' time be valueless, motor trucks will take their place, roads are the arteries of a state.

Then came the mail:

March 8th 1927: No less than 23 whites including three women, my mother, sister and self – gathered at Powell's Creek to greet the first Overland Motor Mail. We now have a trans-continental motor mail service running direct from Oodnadatta in S.A. to Katherine, the railhead of the N.T. This has been a long felt want the pioneers in Central Aussie can now reach Adelaide in 7 days, how different from the old bullock dray days when it used to take weeks and sometimes months to reach the capital. The mail contractors are the well-known and respected firm of Wallis Fogarty of Alice Springs. The popular Bert Wilkinson, a member of the firm, took the opportunity of a run through and acquainted himself with the road, people and conditions on this end. He was highly delighted, surprised and greatly impressed by the lovely country he passed through, and the wonderful possibility as a wool producer in the near future, when railway communications are an established fact. The car is a Graham-Dodge speed wagon, its pilot W. McCoy, a steady reliable chap, and what a driver! Four hundred miles in 2½ days on just a camel pad!

New methods of transport were not the only changes

happening around that time. The first stirrings of social justice were making themselves felt, and a justified repugnance at the old racisms.

At the age of twenty, Elsie wrote what can only be described as a racist rant in the 'Times,' echoing the thought processes of many, but by no means all, of pastoral families at the time. The letter stated the opinion that the Territory would never develop until the blacks were all gone, that they were lazy and generally thieves.

Later, however, Elsie would become a champion of the Reverend John Flynn and his Australian Inland Mission, so her attitudes did change, just as society as a whole was changing.

If there is a dark side to this story, it's the ground-in racism that was unfortunately common at the time. Elsie had probably heard her father and station workers saying similar things. The tirade might even have been provoked by a particular incident.

The roots of this prejudice went deep, perhaps partly to John's German sense of superiority and Esther's Camooweal upbringing. But it also led to a tragic story all too common at the time.

Esther Bohning's two sons to her first husband both grew into strong and knockabout blokes. Jim 'Bull' Bennett, particularly, was well known throughout the Territory.

When Jim took up with an Aboriginal woman called Priscilla (European name) at Helen Springs, and she became pregnant, Esther was furious.

Heavily pregnant, accompanied by her tribal Aboriginal husband, Priscilla escaped into the bush west of Banka Banka Station.

The baby boy was born out there in the wild country, then raised at the Seven Mile, near the site of modern-day Tennant Creek. Jim Bennett visited his son around this time and named him Harry Bennett. Esther, however, was keen to see the child out of the picture and soon had police looking for him.

Little Harry's mother and step dad, however, were determined to keep him safe, even burying him up to his neck in the warm desert sand to keep him hidden when the police were prowling about. If he started to cry they would pile branches around him, then stand around, singing and dancing to cover the sounds of his crying.

After a couple of years out in the deep Tanami, living as nomadic Aborigines, the family arrived at Newcastle Waters, where Harry's parents were given jobs by the local policeman.

At the age of ten or eleven Harry was tricked into going to Birdum (Larrimah) where he was forced into a train carriage full of chained Aboriginal boys. The last time he saw his mother she was running along behind the train, wailing and cutting her head with rocks.

From Larrimah he was taken first to the big city, Darwin, then the Pine Creek Home for Half Caste Boys, and finally an Alice Springs institution where he was kept for years. There he was flogged so hard about the head that he became almost deaf. Later he described how blood and pus would run from his ears after a bashing.

Yet eventually Harry moved back to the Tennant Creek area, and he became first a house boy, then an apprentice butcher. During World War Two he worked for the army, and later in life there was a reconciliation between the Bennett and Bohning parts of the family. Harry met his father several times, but they never became close.

By the early 1930s, Elsie was running the busy homestead at McLaren Creek Station, close to Wauchope, a small centre on the Telegraph Line. This was mainly sandstone country with intrusions of granite, most dramatic at the nearby Devil's Marbles. The homestead was on a rise, surrounded by mulga scrub, with a waterhole on the creek nearby.

Elsie's husband, Fred Harris, according to an interview with one of his workers, was 'cranky in the head.' Not many people, apparently, got on with Fred, though he paid good wages and looked after his men.

Fred swallowed up some other neighbouring properties, including Bonny Creek, and improved the properties with bores and fencing. His main interest was breeding horses, and his stable starred at the Wauchope and Barrow Creek races for thirty years. Elsie delivered the first of their children in the early nineteen-thirties.

In 1935 Elsie was visiting her family home at Helen Springs when her father John did not return from a short overland trip.

> *A sensation was caused in the southern part of the Territory, when word went out that the well-known station owner, Mr Jack Bohning, of Helen Springs, was missing. He had left Mr Charlie Wright's place at dark, to pick up some cattle camped on the way to his own place, but missed the road and went due East past the telegraph line. When he had not returned at day break, the alarm was raised, and the usual band of searchers was quickly scouring the country. The station blacks picked up his tracks and tracked him for over 15 miles, but could not find the man himself. For two days and nights the search was kept up, and hope was almost abandoned when his horse came home, with Mr Bohning, almost all in, sprawled on its neck.*
>
> *After attention from his wife and family and his many friends, Mr Bohning was able to tell his story. It appears that after he had gone to where he thought the cattle camp should be, and was unable to find it in the dark, he decided to go home, but could not find the telegraph line. His horse wanted to turn on several occasions, but Mr Bohning, believing he still knew his position, insisted on going ahead. Finding*

> ultimately that he was lost in the dark, he camped, and when daylight broke he found himself in strange country. The day was extremely hot, and as he was without water, was soon in a bad way. He rode and searched for many miles, but could not find a landmark. At the finish he gave the horse its head, and that at last got him out of his trouble. After going many miles the horse brought him to an old well, with just enough water for them both, and then, with its master in a semi-conscious condition it wended its way home.
>
> The horse, which is a pretty old one, is a great favourite on the station, and is now likely to get the best of attention from the Bohning family.
>
> Mr Bohning is one of the best known cattle men in the Territory, and has been over 40 years in the district. His daughter, Mrs Harris (one time known as the 'Little Bush Maid') along with her two children was on a visit to her parents at the time of the occurrence. Another daughter (Mrs McDonald) is at present living in Darwin.

The war years turned life upside down. The influx of Americans was accompanied by the construction of a real road from North to South, thick with military traffic.

A line was drawn across Australia from just north of Brisbane across the continent. The areas south of the line were considered to be defensible and worth saving. Only a small proportion of Australia's population lived north of Brisbane in those days, and steps were taken to evacuate non-combatants.

In addition to the military trucks on the Stuart Highway, there was also a line of evacuees heading south, in buses, trucks, and private cars.

It was all too much for the ageing Bohnings of Helen Springs, and in 1944 John and Esther sold their beloved station to beef mogul Lord Vestey and retired to Alice Springs.

In 1951 Esther Jenkins became very ill, and Elsie insisted on looking after her at McLaren Creek. Esther died there in 1952, and John outlived her for another six years.

Elsie eventually retired to Coffs Harbour in New South Wales, and went close to seeing out the century. The Helen Springs Bohnings are survived by dozens of descendants, who must be in awe of the world their Jenkins, Bennett and Bohning forebears lived in, not so long ago.

In the words of an amazingly forgiving Harry Bennett:

> *The original pioneering Bohnings and Bennetts have now all passed away. Now I'm the eldest first cousin to all the black and white ones left.*
>
> *There are only three of us coloured ones left now though, the other three passed away. The first son of Esta's (sic) fathered three coloured children. I'm the eldest cousin to the Bohnings today and they reckon they know me, we are proud of one another you know! We're not like the old grandmother! If she was still alive today she would have turned her back on us, but the Bohnings and the Bennetts get on well now.*
>
> *There is no use in continually holding grudges against people, to whom we feel are responsible for what happened to the stolen children. We have to get on with our lives, acknowledge what happened and move on.*

Pearling on the Mona

One of the parts of Charlie Gaunt's life that I would have liked to explore more in Whistler's Bones, but it didn't fit into the story, was his years skippering a pearl lugger out of Broome in the 1890s.

Charlie was able to throw in with a partner, a local businessman called Stanley Piggott, to commission a lugger. The keel was laid by the firm of Chamberlain, down in Fremantle.

Charlie engaged a Japanese diver, a tender (a man to row out with the diver), and a four-man-crew. After provisioning the lugger, now named Mona, Charlie sailed her north to Cygnet Bay, Kings Sound.

In Charlie's words:

> Cygnet Bay in those days was known as the Diver's Graveyard, it had strong currents, deep water and a foul bottom. The shell also was of poor quality – big old shell very rarely carrying good pearls; all Baroque (misshapen pearls worth about twelve pounds per ounce, used by the Chinese to grind into an eye powder).

My diver by the name of Muchisuki was a splendid man but had one fault, being too reckless. He seemed to enjoy gambling with death and at times took great chances. We worked amongst the fleet of luggers, all on good shell. For a neap tide or two nothing unusual happened, until one day a flag was hoisted half-mast on one of Captain Redell's luggers. An accident had happened. Several luggers raced to the scene, to render aid.

My lugger being the first to get to the lugger, my diver called out, "What's the trouble?"

The tender of the other lugger replied, "My diver is fouled and I can't get him up." Getting helmet and face glass on quickly, Muchisuki descended in haste to assist the unfortunate diver. In about five minutes he came up and as soon as we got him on deck he sang out to the tender, "Heave up your anchor and you'll get your man."

The crew rushed to the winch, hove up their anchor and found the diver entangled around the flukes. The goose neck had been broken off the helmet, the diver's skull was smashed in, and he was dead as a door nail. The flukes of the anchor, swinging to and fro had crushed the helmet into a shapeless mass, and then fouled the life line and pipe. The cause of the accident was this: when a diver worked below the vessel drifted after him, the anchor, lowered over, acted as a brake.

The more chain paid out the lower the anchor and slower the progress of the lugger. When the anchor was heaved in the faster the lugger would drift. Now, this diver had been working close to the anchor: which was about a fathom from the bottom and his lines, getting foul of the anchor, through the action of the strong current, he was wound round and round the chain, the flukes swinging backwards and forwards dealing him smashing blows on the head.

One day, Charlie's diver, Muchisuki, stayed below for too long, and he stopped responding to signal tugs on the lifeline.

Myself and the tender heaved on the lifeline and could feel dead weight. Pulling him to the ladder his both hands hanging uselessly down, we knew he was paralysed or dead.

Muchisuki had been diving in water twenty three fathoms deep – more than forty metres. Apart from the tragedy of losing a man Charlie respected, the death put financial pressure on the enterprise.

With no cash to employ another diver Charlie took on the role himself, and the man who once roamed the savannah and open woodland of Australia's north, now worked the bottom of the sea. Up to three miles a day he wandered, collecting shell, and admiring the sea floor.

The submarine scenery in places is almost indescribable. Walking the bottom prospecting for shell the diver will often cover a distance of two or three miles, beds of silver sands, now coming to great fields of waving sea exactly the same as fields of wheat waving with the tide as if a gentle breeze was fanning it. Through those fields and on to beds of beautiful white coral; over them and onto beds of beautiful flowers of many different hues. (When these flowers are brought to the surface and exposed to the air they turn black and have a rank smell).

On over big ironstone ridges, dark caverns, black and forbidding looking, then through a forest of coral cups from the size of a cabbage up to forty feet high, stems two feet through, like champagne glasses. The great feeding ground of fish of all species and the home of some of the best actors of the deep. In some places myriads of fish, red and silver schnapper, white fish and others will swarm around the diver, looking curiously in his face glass.

Charlie had run-ins with eighteen foot-long sharks and huge diamond fish that became entangled in the lines and dragged a helpless driver behind in their panic to be free. Despite the dangerous work, he soon proved that he could do the job profitably.

The first month I brought up about half a ton of pearl shell, and beautiful shell it was. I also got a few pearls.

The Leviathan

The Americans try to take the credit for this, but one of the largest carriages ever made, the 'Leviathan' was actually conceived, designed and built by Australians. Imagine a double-deck horse drawn coach so huge it had separate compartments for men and women, open seating on top and carried sixty-five passengers, sometimes more. 'The Leviathan' was a world first, built in Bendigo by JD Morgan after being commissioned by a group of locals who, unfortunately, ran out of money to pay for it.

Cobb and Co, keen to ease the pressure of trying to transport large numbers of people to the gold diggings, bought the giant coach, and used it on the passenger run between Geelong and Ballarat in Victoria. It was a sensation, with passengers entranced by the novelty. The interior of the coach was decorated with velvet cushions, lush carpets and tapestries.

Drawn by up to eight horses, only an uncommonly strong man could handle the reins. Cobb and Co had only one driver who could handle the task, a master coachman called Ned Devine. Even then, his whip could not reach the leading nags, so with typical colonial ingenuity, he carried a supply of stones to throw at them if they lagged.

A second Leviathan was built, but the giant coaches fell into disuse as railways took over the routes. They were apparently sold several times, one transporting shearers around the sheds in New South Wales then ending up in Western Australia. The other was shipped to Adelaide and eventually scrapped.

Lost

It was May 1885, and twelve-year-old Clara Crosby was boarding with a local family at Yellingbo, Victoria, when she decided to visit her mother, who lived some two kilometres away.

Setting off across paddocks and bushland, Clara was seen by several locals, including the publican, as she left town. She failed to reach her destination.

By nightfall the police had been alerted. Troopers, black-trackers and local bushmen combined to comb the area, but heavy rain obliterated any tracks. After days of intensive searching the party dispersed, and it was assumed that Clara had died in the heavy scrub that surrounded the town.

Days of grieving passed by, and slowly the little town began to recover from what seemed like a senseless tragedy. Then, three full weeks after Clara had first wandered off, two road workers were looking for a horse in thick scrub far from the town, when they heard a human-like cry.

In the hollow trunk of a dead tree they found a starving, naked girl, streaked with lacerations and so weak she could not stand. Clara sobbed with relief as they wrapped her in their jackets and took her back to their camp for food and warmth. By nightfall she was recovering at the Woori Yallock Hotel, with her mother in attendance. Within days she was being hailed across the country as a miracle.

Clara had taken a wrong turn and walked blindly into the scrub. She had lost her clothes trying to cross the near-freezing waters of Cockatoo Creek, and kept herself alive on water and leaves, hanging her petticoat over the opening of her hollow tree to keep the warmth in.

Later, a Melbourne waxworks induced Clara to recount her story for a fee, and over time, some 150 000 people paid money to hear her story. Later she was married, unfortunately into an abusive relationship.

Well known painter, Frederick McCubbin heard the story in 1886. He was, at the time, in one of his 'bush camps' in company with other artists like Arthur Streeton and Charles Conder at a farm near Box Hill. His painting Lost (main image) was based on Clara's experiences, and was followed a few years later by a companion piece, called Found.

The Lake Nash Drought and a Push for Water.

In 1889 Charlie Gaunt was working on Lake Nash Station, first breaking horses and then as a stockman.

Lake Nash Station was, at the time Charlie arrived there, still under the ownership of John Costello, brother of Patsy Durack's wife Mary and the reason for the delay to the drive on the Limmen River years earlier. John's pride and joy, Valley of Springs Station had, by this stage, been abandoned.

John Costello's son Martin was managing Lake Nash. Back in Goulburn in his teens Martin had felt himself called to Holy Orders, but quit after a few months. Life on a cattle station must have appealed, and his father had plans for Martin to eventually take over as owner. He was, according to Charlie: 'About twenty-five years of age, a splendid type of an Irish Australian, a chip off the old block; only lacking experience; a thoroughbred and a perfect gentleman.'

When the horse-breaking was done Charlie signed on as stockman, but things on the station were dire. The 1889 wet season had been light, and in 1890 the rain didn't come at all. This was Charlie's story of a mad dash to a big waterhole in the Rankin River, attempting to save the remaining cattle.

Costello decided that they had to try something – gathering up the strongest cattle and trying for the nearest permanent water – the Big Hole on the Rankin River, eighty miles away.

They sent a dray and horses on ahead, and mustered every animal they could find and set off.

The heat at that time, January, was terrific, and the dry storms made it worse with the hot winds. We had great difficulty getting the mob away from that charnel house and lake of liquid mud, but once they got going they strung up the river almost without any urging. The day wore on and night came and still those perishing cattle moved slowly along.

Lake Nash in better times (NT Library)

After a day and a night of travelling, they reached Austral Downs station, which had been abandoned to the drought. With just twenty miles to go now Charlie rode across to check the station tanks and found enough water to keep the horses going.

At least the horses had drunk their fill as they followed the thirst-maddened cattle down the left branch of the Rankin River. The sun was getting higher, however, and the heat intensifying.

> *The cattle at the rear now began to drop and die, but doggedly through that long day the big body of the cattle kept following that spirit 'Further Still.' The only sound they made was a low moaning. As evening came I rode up*

on the side to see how the lead was getting along, accompanied by Mick Scanlon. We rode a full six miles before we reached it. All along the line we noticed cattle dropping and dying but yet that line piled up the empty spaces. Great strong bullocks formed the lead and you dared not go near them. They were thoroughly thirst-maddened.

It was now dark and we rode close to the lead, when a demented bullock charged my horse, knocking it down and throwing me out of the saddle. We were amongst the infuriated animals and didn't know it, the night being inky black.

I jumped up and shinnied up a tree close by and yelled to Mick to save himself, telling him I was alright, and that I'd stay in the tree fork till daylight. Mick soon got out of that maddened line of cattle and I saw him no more that night. All night long those thirst crazed cattle passed under that tree and I, sitting in the fork, hardly able to keep awake, waited for the dawn.

When, at last, daylight came, I got out of the tree and walked over to my horse. He was lying dead with a great wound behind the shoulder having bled to death. Removing the saddle and bridle I threw them on my back and started to walk up the river. After walking about four miles, dodging cattle, at last I struck the Big Hole and the camp. I was, like those stricken cattle – perishing for a drink. I had had no *water since the day before at midday.*

What a tragic scene was being enacted around that waterhole! Maddened cattle, some blind with thirst, moaning and walking through the water, being too far gone to drink. Up the bank they went and wandered out on the downs. After the drought broke we found that some of them had wandered six miles out from the river before dying.

The tail-enders drifted in and these represented the last of the living. Our men were now all in camp and we gladly sat down to a hot breakfast. Camped on a high bank overlooking the water we were in full view of that theatre. Only about five hundred head were left out of four thousand and were the remnant of a herd of fifteen thousand. The Big Hole where the cattle were, was on Avon Downs country, and John Affleck, manager of Avon, charged young Costello £100 per month for the right to use the water and surrounding country. It was a most unneighbourly and cowardly action to a now ruined brother stockman, but John Affleck was, a hard, hungry and mean Scotsman and he well knew that Costello had to accede to his terms. It was especially mean on account of the country being idle and not used by the Avon Downs people.

We, spectators of that terrible drama of crazed cattle wandering around the banks of that waterhole, piling into it, and gorging themselves. In some cases animals staggering out on the banks and lying down to die overgorged, the water flowing out of their nostrils as they drew their last breath.

On the bank nearest the camp some horses were standing and amongst them was a magnificent chestnut horse young Costello had brought from Goulburn. This animal was the young fellow's pride. A maddened bullock, staggering along the creek saw the horse, made a desperate charge at it and tipped the entrails out of him. Martin Costello said, 'Oh, my God, my horse.'

And the tears slowly coursed down his face. The long pent up agony that the young fellow had gone and was going through was at last broken by this incident. Fate had dealt him a cruel blow. He got up, walked behind the dray, sat down, and with his head resting on his arms and knees he had the dejected attitude of a heartbroken man. Every man around the breakfast table felt the position keenly and there was a lump in everyone's throat. I know there was one in mine.

In the beginning of March; the arch fiend 'Drought' was killed by one of the heaviest wet seasons known for years and we collected the remnants (five hundred head of cattle) of the Lake Nash herd and went back to reform the station.

The Man with a Mission

The year was 1882, and the sheets were wet with blood and sweat as the young woman fought to deliver her third child. The baby was born sickly and weak. Even worse, the midwife could not stop the new mother from bleeding. It was soon obvious that she was dying.

A two-year-old boy was brought into the room, so his dying mother could see him one last time. He must have been deeply affected, although seemingly too young to understand. Who could have guessed that one day this child's achievements would see his image gracing Australia's $20 note!

The boy's schoolteacher father was unable to cope after the loss of his wife, and the boy was sent to be raised by his aunt in Sydney until he was five. At that age he returned to his father in Snake Gully, near Ballarat.

"Good to have you home John," said his father, ruffling his hair. "Us Flynns have to stick together."

After leaving school, John followed in his father's footsteps, enrolling as a pupil-teacher, but also studying theology through the Presbyterian Church. His first appointment as a pastor was to Dunesk Mission in the Northern Flinders

Ranges, and his affinity for the bush led to the Church commissioning him to visit the Northern Territory and assess the needs of the people who lived there.

The result of that report was that Flynn was given responsibility for the newly formed Australian Inland Mission. He organised "patrols" of ministers on horseback, based in Oodnadatta, Port Hedland, Broome and Cloncurry. He set up nursing hostels in Port Hedland, Hall's Creek, Maranboy (near Katherine) and Alice Springs.

John was desperate to help solve the "tyranny of distance." A badly injured drover at Wave Hill, for example, faced a journey that might stretch to weeks to reach medical help in Katherine, by which time they were often dead or suffering from gangrene.

Two relatively new inventions were rattling around the back of John's mind. One was the aeroplane, and the other was the two-way radio. After a long testing phase, and years of gathering support from various state governments and the church itself, the Australian Aerial Medical Service was born.

Busy to the point of obsession, John also found time for the good things in life. He was a passionate photographer, and though he had no time for romance in his early years, he married his secretary, Jean Baird, at the age of fifty-one.

The effect of the Flying Doctor on inland Australia can't be overestimated. Thousands of lives have been saved, many of them the children of remote families. Even now, the Royal Flying Doctor Service operates sixty-eight aircraft, and assists a quarter of a million people each year through clinics, telehealth services, and emergency visits.

John Flynn died of cancer, in 1951. Speaking at the funeral his former senior padre, Kingsley Partridge, said, "Across the lonely places of the land he planted kindness, and from the hearts of those who call those places home, he gathered love." Not a bad epitaph for a man who saw his mother die in childbirth and pursued a dream, believing that medical help could reach every Australian, no matter where they lived.

James 'Shearblade' Martin

So often, Australian historical figures who advanced the cause of the British Empire fill the pages of our history books. But a true Australian revolutionary who helped command an 'army' of ten thousand men and threatened to take over Queensland by force of arms doesn't even rate a Wikipedia page.

James Martin was working as a boundary rider when he first got his hands on a copy of Karl Marx's Communist Manifesto. He was thunderstruck by the possibilities. He carried the book everywhere while he absorbed every word. He then moved on to other socialist writers such as Bellamy and Nordeau.

A dream was born, to make Australia a worker's republic, owned by the people.

In 1891, while shearing shed after shearing shed was burned to the ground by rampaging shearers, Martin hurried from town to town, enlisting recruits and trying to convince strike breakers to change sides. In Barcaldine he addressed a crowd where he announced that it was time to move against the Queen, who he referred to as 'Old Mother Brown.'

'What we want is a revolution and a republic,' he said. 'If the amalgamated miners are prepared to back us, we are prepared to take the colony. I have a petition in my swag for electoral reform, but the only petition I believe in is 10,000 resolute bushmen behind 10,000 shear blades.' His numbers were not inflated. 8000 strikers were living in at least forty camps across Queensland, and thousands more were living independently or at home.

Almost as furious about Martin's disrespect to the Queen as his threat to conquer Queensland, a team of policemen were set on the trail of the man now known as James 'Shearblade' Martin. On the day of his arrest he was carrying a revolver and seventy cartridges. This fact did not impress the judge. He was sentenced to two years in prison for sedition, and taken to the dreaded St Helena Island, off the mouth of the Brisbane River. Known variously as 'the hell hole of the Pacific' and 'Queensland's Inferno,' Martin served two years in that gaol, suffering mercilessly under the lash and terrible conditions.

Released at the end of his sentence, Martin soon turned up in Charleville, taking control of the Australian Workers Union there, just in time for the next round of the Shearer's Wars in 1894. He marched a small army to Winton, where the strike action was centred. Terrorising and converting scab labour was the number one activity, and Martin was involved in the burning of at least three woolsheds.

This was harsh, but bear in mind that the pastoralists had again banded together to set shearers' pay below what was considered a living wage. These men were fighting for the right of their families to eat.

For the burning of Ayrshire Downs woolshed Martin was ultimately charged with arson and sentenced to fifteen years at hard labour. They transported him on a steamer, padlocked to his bunk, to Townsville's Stewart Creek Gaol, where he was placed in solitary confinement, in tropical heat, for three months. Later that year he was taken back to Brisbane's Boggo Road, and ultimately to his old prison at Saint Helena Island, where he worked, for a time, as librarian, bootmaker, and cook.

Petitioned for early release, by members of the original jury, and 1500 members of the public, Martin and his co-accused served only four and a half years. This was the end of James Martin's dreams of a worker's state in Australia, however. After his release James 'Shearblade' Martin went to join the revolution in Paraguay, where his side had much better success than they did in Australia.

The Town on the Flood Plain

Australia's worst flood drowned one third of the population of Gundagai in 1852. The town was originally built on low-lying areas around a natural river crossing and Morley's Creek. The inhabitants were used to being cut off by floodwaters, taking refuge in their lofts when the water rose.

Yet on June 24 1852, the rain kept falling and the river kept rising. By late that night, two metres of water had inundated or swept away many of the houses and huge floating trees were pummelling what was left.

When the sun rose the next day, eighty-nine people were dead, and dozens more were left clinging to trees and rooftops. Rowboats were useless in the swift water.

Yarri, Long Jimmy and Jacky Jacky, local Aboriginal men who had been warning Gundagai residents for years that their town would be washed away, launched their bark canoes in a desperate rescue attempt. Over the next two days, with the river now one mile across where the town used to be, at least forty, perhaps sixty more people were saved by the efforts of these Indigenous boatmen. Long Jimmy died from exposure after his efforts on the flooded river. Yarri and Jacky Jacky were rewarded with bronze medallions.

The town was eventually rebuilt on higher ground, but it still suffers from the occasional inundation, with water entering the main street in 2012, thankfully without loss of life.

John Moore Gaunt and the St Kilda Years

If you've read Whistler's Bones, or intend to, here's some background on drover and adventurer Charlie Gaunt's early life.

Charlie Gaunt's father was named John Moore Gaunt, the son of a Leeds barrister and alderman. John arrived on the *Tippoo Saib* in 1852, twenty one years old, and full of ambition and charm. He was part of the first wave of goldfields immigrants, fired-up by stories of men picking nuggets off the surface at Mount Alexander and Ballarat.

By the time John reached the fields the plum claims were already pegged, but there were millions of tonnes of alluvial gravel still to be panned. He must have had some success with the sluice box, for in 1853 he purchased 40 acres of land at Yarram Yarram, near Mornington, in partnership with his brother. This he disposed of in the next few years, but then, in 1857, he took up a parcel of seventy acres. John, it seems, never set eyes on the block, but the land was leased out, with an annual rent of £20.

By 1856 John was living in Park Street, St Kilda, working for the Victorian government. Four years later, his big break came. He was appointed to the post of acting Gold Receiver in the town of Inglewood.

Life in Inglewood suited John, and he made a life-long

friend, a young doctor, around the same age, called Henry Hayton Radcliffe. Together they joined the Aurora Lodge of the Freemasons, a fraternity of Anglican businessmen organised into lodges: the members of which advance through a series of guilds. The lodges offered networking opportunities similar to modern day Lions and Rotary Clubs.

Augusta Fuller and her sister Charlotte were by then eligible young women, living in the area. Augusta was in her late teens, Charlotte her early twenties.

John Gaunt was playing cricket for the Inglewood XI one fine Saturday, making a sensible thirty-six runs before tea. At the break he was presented to Augusta by mutual friends.

'I enjoyed watching you bat,' she said.

'If I'd known such a presentable lady was watching I would have bashed out a century.'

After tea John returned to the crease and was clean bowled first ball!

John Gaunt was fifteen years older than Augusta, and must have made her heart skip a few beats. After all, in 1862 he had been added to the roll of Magistrates for the State of Victoria. He appeared to offer stability and financial well-being, qualities that must have been irresistible to Augusta.

The wedding followed three months later, on the second of December 1863. The Reverend William Chalmers conducted the ceremony. Anna Maria gave her daughter away and John's mate and brother-in-law Henry was best man.

The future seemed bright. John and Augusta were essentially compatible. Both from strong Church of England families, with intelligent, professional forbears, they were committed to their family and looked forward to raising children together.

John and Augusta's eldest son, William, was born in Inglewood, near Bendigo, yet the rising star of John's career was faltering. He formally resigned from the roll of magistrates in the Colony of Victoria. No reason was recorded, and he was soon being shunted between lesser roles.

The family moved to Melbourne, and were living at Argyle Street, St Kilda, on December the 6th, 1865, when the couple gave birth to a second male child. They named him Charles Edward Gaunt.

John Gaunt had a dry and cutting Yorkshireman's sense of humour, and had always been keen on a drink or two. Increasing overindulgence meant that cracks soon appeared in his life, both personally and professionally. He was posted to Bairnsdale, Gippsland, first as an acting Lands Officer, then as Clerk of Courts, but his fondness for whisky made it difficult for him to carry out his duties to the satisfaction of his superiors. It was also tough on his family, for he was a hard man, prone to bouts of violence.

John and Augusta's first daughter, Harriet, died after just four weeks and four days of life. The cause was listed on her birth certificate as 'Debility from Birth.' Watching her waste away must have taken a heavy emotional toll.

Tired of the constant shifts, the family soon elected to stay put while John went off for yet another relieving or short term position. These years were spent in rented houses in St Kilda and Prahran, Melbourne – Fitzroy Street, Robe Street, Octavia Street, and Punt Road, Prahan.

St Kilda was still in the second phase of its development. The rough port town, and the seaside coffee shop suburb were still in the future.

As historian John Butler Cooper noted of the city at in the 1860s and 70s:

'St Kilda was a conservative, homely and very English place ... the prevailing sentiment was English, for most of the fathers, and mothers had been emigrants. They formed the backbone of the community of St Kilda, and gave the place its character.'

Family events became shared milestones. When Charlie was six years old the house next door to theirs in Octavia Street caught fire in the early hours of the morning, burning to the ground while the boys, their father and the fire brigade worked tirelessly to prevent the blaze spreading. All the Gaunt family's outbuildings were lost, including presumably, the outside dunny, but the rented house was saved.

In those days Prahran was mainly open paddock, and

wandering cows were the cause of many an argument. The Gaunt family kept at least some livestock, for in August 1868, John Moore Gaunt was fined five shillings for having an 'errant' goat.

Every Sunday, the family dressed up and walked to the All Saints Church in Chapel Street, East St Kilda. Faced with Tasmanian bluestone, it was the largest parish church south of the equator, able to squeeze in 1400 worshippers. Weekly services were run by the founding father, Reverend John Herbert Gregory, who had given up a career in law to take Holy Orders.

The children attended the schoolhouse attached to the church, and for secondary schooling a Grammar School opened in 1871 on the corner of Chapel Street and Dandenong Road. Fees were high – up to three guineas per term for day students, but the family managed.

Two more girls were born. Marion arrived in 1871 and Ellen in 1874. Both were baptised at St Kilda by the Reverend Gregory. The church was a constant, steadying influence, as was a large extended family. John's brother, James Richardson Gaunt, who had immigrated a few years after John, visited often. He had a much more adventurous spirit than John, and even played a small part in the Eureka Rebellion on the Ballarat goldfields.

Augusta's mother Maria was living in Mair St, Ballarat, and would also have been a regular house guest. George remained a loveable ruffian, in and out of trouble in the same area.

The Gaunt family's closest friendship was still, however, with Augusta's sister Charlotte, and her husband, Henry Radcliffe. Their years in Inglewood together had made them close, sharing the excitements of childbirths, and the sadness of Charlotte losing her daughter Ella at just nine months, while the men chased success in their fledgling careers.

Change was coming, however, very little of it for the better.

John's drinking went through cycles of wild excess followed by sober periods that might last for months or even years.

Just one dram, Aggie. That's all I'll have …

James Richardson Gaunt moved to Queensland, setting himself up as a businessman in partnership with a man called Henry Britcher, in Adavale, west of Charleville. Henry Britcher's brother George would later feature tragically in one of Charlie's adventures.

John publicly forswore booze, and declared himself a teetotaller in 1877. There were reports that he had joined the Good Templar Crusaders. This 'new leaf' brought results, and John's final government appointment was to Sandhurst, as Bendigo was then known, to perform the duties of Paymaster and Receiver.

The family settled into a house rented from the All Saints Parish, on Rowan Street, within walking distance of the Government offices where John worked, and also the Masonic Hall. The children thrived in the new town. William and Charlie attended the Church of England school run by the fiery Reverend Croxton next to their parish church, named All Saints just like the one at home in St Kilda.

All Saints Sandhurst was a gothic edifice of yellow sandstone blocks, squat and sacred-looking. It had narrow arched windows fitted with stained glass images of the saints in dull colours.

On Sundays John, Augusta, William and Charlie sat together in the hard pews of the church, while the girls scampered off to Sunday school. John was a bloated and increasingly tragic figure, now suffering from dropsy, his puffy limbs and neck the subject of laughter and jokes behind his back.

Twelve months later, in 1879, his dropsy worsening, and entering the final stages of alcoholism, John Gaunt was dismissed from government service for 'gross neglect of duty.' At around the same time, John's father back in Yorkshire died, and he expected a large inheritance.

The Bendigo Advertiser reported in May 1879 that J.M. Gaunt was the recipient of a considerable sum of money from his father's will and that he had announced his intention, should his health permit, to travel by sea to England at the first opportunity. John was, according to this report, suffering from 'colonial fever' and needed a sea voyage to clear it from his system.

John died a year later, at the age of fifty, principally from cirrhosis of the liver. He was buried in the old Bendigo cemetery, and no trace of a headstone remains. It seems certain that by then his old employers had turned their back on him, and there was no government funeral.

With two pounds and five shillings of rent overdue, and John's money tied up until the will could be probated, the church wardens of All Saints Parish acted quickly. With full legal backing, they ejected the family from the Rowan Street house, forcing a fire sale of furniture and effects; everything the family had collected over the years.

Augusta and her four children found themselves out on the street. Marion was nine years old, Ellen only six.

Charlotte and Henry (also the executor of John's will) came to the rescue, and the broken family planned a move to Ballarat, at least until some money from John's will became available to them.

The family was not destitute. John's estate included ownership of the seventy-acre block at Mornington he had bought with his brother, (which would later cause a serious feud and numerous court cases). He also had fifty-one pounds to his credit in his account at the Commercial Bank when he died, presumably the remains of his inheritance. Yet, he had racked up a number of debts. Crabbe and Kirby, solicitors, executors of the will, placed a notice in the Bendigo Advertiser calling for particulars of all claims against the estate of John Gaunt to be made by August, 1880. These small debts totalled some seventy-two pounds.

The real salvation was a life insurance policy valued at three hundred and fifty pounds; John's gift to the family he had let down so badly. Overall, Augusta and the children received just under four hundred, enough to buy a cheap house, but not enough to invest at interest and survive on.

But that money was a long time coming. Augusta tried desperately to hold the family together. The boys, however

– William and Charlie – had other ideas.

William, like his grandfather on his mother's side, planned for a career in medicine. With a favourable response to an application to study at Edinburgh University, Scotland, he booked his passage to the United Kingdom.

Charlie, barely fifteen years old, spent his share of his father's money on a horse and saddle. He taught himself to ride on barren goldfields hills and over long hours in the saddle he discovered that he liked horses and they liked him.

And that, pretty much, is where Whistler's Bones starts off.

The Girder that Wouldn't Fit

Things were tough in the NSW North Coast forests in 1907. All the cedar had been cut years earlier, prices for hardwoods had slumped, and the best way to make money was by shaping girders and sleepers.

Tamban Forest woodcutter Bob Cooper was lucky-enough to snag an order for a huge 86 foot (26 m) girder from a Sydney construction company. Bob selected a giant ironbark tree, and skilfully felled it along the hill contour.

After trimming off the branches Bob used a string line blackened with charcoal as a straight-edge, and over days of back-breaking labour with a broad axe, finally squared the girder into the required 16 inch (400mm) square dimensions.

Promising a party for his friends and helpers on the basis of a forthcoming big cheque, Bob followed the girder as a bullock team dragged it down to Clybucca Creek, from which point it was punted up the Macleay River to Frederickton Wharf.

Moored at the wharf was the graceful three masted topsail schooner, Alma Doepel, of one hundred and thirty one tons displacement. One look at the boat was enough to tell that the girder was far too big for the hold.

'No worries,' the captain said cheerfully, 'we'll get it aboard somehow.'

Bob had some business in Kempsey to attend to, but returned a couple of hours later to see that the Alma Doepel was still at the wharf, with no sign of the big girder.

'You got it in the hold?' Bob exclaimed. 'How the hell did you do that?'

'Easy,' the captain told him. 'We just cut it in half. Then it fitted nicely.'

History doesn't record how Bob took that news. But apparently the party planned in celebration of a big cheque was cancelled.

(Interestingly, the Alma Doepel, originally built in Bellingen, survives today as a sail training ship, and is berthed at No 2 Victoria Dock Melbourne undergoing a refit.)

AUSTRALIANS AT WAR

The McGree Brothers of Taylors Arm

John, Michael and Patrick McGree were raised on their parents' farm on the Mid-North coast of NSW. All three answered the call to arms in 1915. The ANZAC battalions were forming up, and the brothers were determined to have their chance at glory.

Their mother, Bridget Sullivan, had married Irishman James McGree in St Augustine's Church, Longford, Tasmania in 1874. The young couple moved north and took up a selection on Hickey's Creek near Kempsey. Life was tough, but like most good Catholic families they welcomed children, bringing twelve boys and girls into the world over a twenty-five-year period.

Patrick, the oldest of the three McGree boys who served, was a born adventurer. He headed off to New Zealand at an early age, living in Waiapo and Gisborne. He kept in touch with his Australian family via mail and occasional visits.

In 1914, when war broke out, Patrick was 31 years old, yet he signed on with the Wellington Infantry, New Zealand Expeditionary Force. Michael crossed the Tasman Sea to join his brother, but was waylaid by an unscheduled love affair. He married his Kiwi girl, Nellie, just before heading off for intensive training in Egypt.

John, still at home on the farm outside Taylors Arm, was 22 when he joined up in 1915. He was a small, wiry man, weighing just 58 kg, and of average height. In fact, none of the McGree boys were tall, but were all as tough as nails, with brilliant blue eyes and Irish charm. The doctor examining Michael for his enlistment described him as having a 'grand constitution.'

Patrick and Michael, though assigned to different units, both took their place amongst the bloody heroes of the ANZAC landings at Gallipoli. Both survived the early days of suicide charges on the well-entrenched Turks, but natural attrition took its toll. Patrick was killed on August 8, 1915, in the defence of a hill called Chunuk Bair.

Michael was wounded in the last days of the Gallipoli campaign, and was evacuated to the Fulham Military Hospital in England. His recuperation was slow, and he endured hospitalisation for almost six months before being returned to his unit, judged as fit to serve in the hellish trenches of France.

On the 28th of July 1916 that 'tough little bastard' John McGree was one of thousands sent in human waves against the German trenches at the Battle of the River Somme. He was shot in the chest and back. He was still alive when he reached the field hospital, but died within twenty-four hours. He was buried at the nearby Warloy-Baillon Military Cemetery.

James and Bridget received the usual telegram from Base Records in Melbourne informing them of John's death: a message just fourteen words long. Losing one son was hard enough. The loss of a second must have been hard to bear.

Bridget penned a desperate letter back to Base Records.

Dear Sir

Please could you give me any information about the death of my son Pte John A McGree No. 3888, who died of

> *wounds in France ... I would like to know the name of the hospital where he died, also if he was seriously wounded or what caused his death. What were his last words and where is he buried? Please send reply as soon as possible.*
>
> *B. McGree,*

Taylor's Arm, via Macksville

Five months passed before she received any additional information: a kind letter informing her of the nature of John's wounds and the name of the hospital and cemetery. John's personal effects also arrived in the mail: one religious medallion, three handkerchiefs, two brushes, a cap comforter, one photograph and a notebook.

By July 1918, the surviving brother, Michael McGree, was a veteran of three years of the most terrible warfare mankind had ever known. On the morning of July 18, 1918, just months before the end of the war, his company were ordered to attack a fortified German trench at Gommecourt Wood, France. Running into a hail of lead, Michael was killed in action, just a few kilometres away from the site of his brother John's death, two years earlier.

Their father, James McGree died at the age of 86, in 1928. Bridget lived on until she was 87, a highly respected local pioneer, and a matriarch of the Laverty, Brock, and McGree families. She died in 1940 and was buried in Macksville cemetery.

The strength she must have had to shoulder the grief of three lost sons is a testament to the spirit of not just the Anzacs, but their families.

The Nackeroos

Did a regiment made up of Aussie bushmen and Indigenous soldiers stop the Japanese from invading in World War Two?

Australia's North West Mobile Force, better known as NORFORCE, are a regiment of tough Aussie soldiers, mostly born in the Top End. Designed primarily as a surveillance unit, as well as a stay-behind force if we're ever invaded, they are trained to survive indefinitely, live off the bush and pass on intelligence to the ADF command.

NORFORCE, however, dates back to World War Two. Its original incarnation was called the North Australian Observation Unit, better known as the Nackeroos, formed when the Japanese invasion of Australia was a real possibility. Most members of the unit were practised horsemen and bushmen. They used horses, small boats, vehicles and even donkeys for transport. A large proportion were, and remain, indigenous.

Most historians now believe that by 1943 the Japanese had rejected the idea of invading Australia, but air attacks on Darwin, Katherine and Broome made it seem imminent at the time. There were other worrying signs – a network of Japanese spies in Northern Australia, and a cache of Japanese oil drums found near the mouth of the Roper River.

So how did the Nackeroos scare the Japanese away in World War Two?

Lieutenant Colonel Bill Stanner, commander of the Nackeroos, came up with a unique plan. Two-man units were dispersed across remote parts of the Top End with hundreds of powerful radio sets. By broadcasting daily reports that greatly exaggerated their numbers, these mobile units were credited with making the enemy believe that they faced a large number of troops, when in fact the Nackeroos numbered just a few hundred.

There is evidence that four Japanese officers on a spy boat landed on the remote Kimberley coast in 1944 to investigate reports of huge naval bases being established in the area, all fuelled by reports from the Nackeroos' radio networks.

We now know that Japanese estimates of how many soldiers would be required to invade Australia rose from three divisions to ten divisions (150 000 troops and 2 million tonnes of shipping to transport them). What made them change their calculations so dramatically?

It's possible that the Nackeroos were behind this vast increase in estimates of required force, thus making the invasion unviable. Either way, the NAOU plan to outfox the Japanese was an interesting and little known aspect of the Pacific War, and we may still be reaping the benefits today.

The Stone-throwing Battle of the Margaret River

In 1880, Australia's borders were open, with no quarantine, and no immigration controls. Chinese miners had been flooding into the Territory goldfields for years. The Margaret River goldfields, north of Pine Creek, were worked by two rival Chinese factions, one from Hong Kong and the other, Macao. When they weren't attacking each other with muzzle-loaders and shovels, they united against the Australian miners.

In late August, 1880, a young digger by the name of Fred Stone asked a storekeeper called Ah See to look after a bag of his wash-dirt overnight to save him carrying it back to his claim. For some reason the request enraged the Chinese man, who responded by pushing the Australian out onto the track.

Punches were thrown, and the furious storekeeper shouted for help from his countrymen, who came running from all directions. Picking up stones, they pelted Fred from all sides until he broke and ran. His Australian comrades, up at the camp, were greeted with the sight of their mate running flat out towards them, pursued by a mob of two hundred rock-throwing Chinese.

What choice did the white diggers have? Filling their

own pockets with rocks they rushed to their mate's defence, pouring a highly accurate barrage of missiles down on the Chinese. Meanwhile, the only policeman within cooee, Constable Lucanus, ran back and forth trying to quell the riot. He eventually succeeded, but not before he too had been peppered with rocks in the body and legs.

An eyewitness to the fight, a reporter from the Northern Territory Times and Gazette wrote:

'Some of the incidents of the battle were amusing. One powerful young European came to the front and intended to throw stones in return, but he became a splendid object for the enemy; and instead of throwing, he found himself sufficiently occupied in avoiding the missiles. He admitted himself (that) it was a most unsatisfactory method of fighting.'

The smallest white man there was apparently the best rock chucker, being described as a human Gatling Gun, causing carnage amongst the 'enemy.' Not every man was armed with rocks: two diggers with rifles, and a local Aboriginal man called Billy Muck with his tomahawk, stood by, watching in case things got out of hand.

In the end, five of the most violent of the Chinese were arrested, taken to the 'shackle' and tried for affray. Within a few years the area was mainly worked out and abandoned. Interestingly, a portion of the Margaret River goldfields has recently been designated as a public fossicking area.

The Siege of Dagworth

The shearers' strikes of the 1890s flared dangerously close to open warfare. It was a bitter struggle, with no sympathies between the conflicting sides. As one old timer recalled:

> *The wonder is that the strike and its attendant disturbances did not end in civil war. Since the Eureka Stockade, Australia has never experienced such a period of industrial upheaval, with the shearers in thousands armed with rifles, and military and police parading the districts of the central-west with an armament that included Gatling guns. There were many clashes and sensational incidents. Wool sheds were burnt on some stations, and considerable damage to property ensued before the struggle ended.*

The reasons for the strikes were many, but were mainly related to pay and conditions. Shearers were paid just fifteen to seventeen shillings for every hundred sheep they shore, and were often expected to live rough while at the shed. Shearers also objected to being forced to shear wet fleeces.

Troopers at Dagworth Station during the Shearers' Strike in 1894

In 1894, a heavily fortified woolshed near Kyuna, Queensland, was bristling with guns, manned by special constables and station employees. It came under attack from a dozen determined shearers. Bullets flew in both directions, but the defenders kept themselves hidden behind stout log barricades.

One of the shearers crept forward with a kerosene bottle and used it as a crude Molotov cocktail to set fire to the shed. The defenders were forced to withdraw, but the arsonist hadn't reckoned on the presence of 140 sheep in the yards. All were burned away to a terrible death. So ended the Battle of Dagworth.

The next day the squatter and the special constables who had been in the siege rode down to a nearby waterhole, where they found the body of Sam Hoffmeister, the man who started the fire. Racked with guilt he had shot himself during the night.

Interestingly, Banjo Patterson, then a lawyer hired to bring the warring parties together, visited Dagworth in the aftermath of the siege. Soon afterwards he made that historic visit to Combo waterhole, near Winton, with the station manager MacPherson, where they surprised an old swagman killing and dressing a station sheep.

It's almost certain that the suicide death of Hoffmeister made its way into the lyrics of Waltzing Matilda, a story of independent spirit and resistance to authority.

The Battle of Long Tan

The Battle of Long Tan is remembered for the bravery and sacrifice of D Company, 6 RAR, and the effective implementation of Australian weapons and tactics.

In 1966, 1 ATF (the First Australian Task Force) took responsibility for a large and tactically important slice of Vietnam. It was a tough gig: Phuoc Tuy Province had a long frontage to the South China Sea, including the strategic port Vung Tau near the mouth of the Saigon River. The geography included coastal mangrove swamps, flat lowlands, hills, and mountainous country in the far north east. The Viet Cong had supply routes and bases across the province.

Brigadier David Jackson, commander of the Task Force, chose to site the Australian base at a rubber plantation called Nui Dat. It was a provocative move, right on a Viet Cong supply route, and holding a commanding position over the central part of the province.

Villages within mortar range of the proposed base were cleared and relocated, and work began in May 1966. Viet Cong resistance was fierce and numerous small-scale battles were fought in the establishment phase. Jackson insisted on strong fixed defences to negate fears of a full-scale Viet Cong attack on the base.

Early in the morning of the 17th of August, 1966, base personnel were looking forward to a concert by visiting performers Col Joye and Little Pattie, when the first mortar round dropped in from VC baseplate positions to the East. For twenty-two minutes the bombardment continued. One man was killed and twenty-four wounded.

The next morning B Company, 6RAR, were ordered out through the wire to find the perpetrators. They had little trouble locating the Vietcong fire positions, but the enemy had withdrawn, and none were encountered.

On the morning of the 18th, it was D Company's turn. They patrolled out past B Company's position, intent on following the tracks left by the enemy. Splitting into their four platoons, they followed two cart tracks leading off to the east into a thick rubber plantation.

It was a dull and frightening environment in which to operate, with evenly spaced rubber trees in all directions – good visibility along the rows, but only a few metres at certain angles. Even so, at this stage the 108 men of D Company still believed that they were facing a band of local VC, who had most likely left the area.

At 1540 that afternoon, 11 Platoon came under fire through the rubber from a six-man enemy patrol. Fire was exchanged, and, as they returned to the route, more contacts followed. Before long, the Australians were heavily engaged. 11 Platoon found themselves all but surrounded by uniformed troops firing AK47 rifles.

The rest of the company hurried forward to assist, but they had underestimated the enemy. The company was being encircled by a battalion strength force that included the Viet Cong's 275 Regiment, and elements of the North Vietnamese Army. To make matters worse, heavy monsoon rain began to fall.

11 Platoon's commander was an early casualty, and with

one third of the men down, the tattered remnants withdrew to join their comrades. The company commander, Major Smith, brought his beleaguered men together and formed a strong defensive perimeter.

There, deep in the rubber trees, as darkness fell and the rain poured down, less than a hundred men, many of them wounded, withstood wave after wave of attacks from an enemy armed with automatic weapons. But the Aussies chose their targets well, and their SLRs were reliable and built to perform in any conditions. Again and again those Lithgow-made rifles barked, and the bolts slid forwards and backwards sending their deadly load into the seemingly limitless attackers. Using field radios the Australians called brutally precise artillery fire down on the Viet Cong positions. The use of artillery in this battle was the decisive factor.

By 1700 the men, lying or kneeling shoulder to shoulder in the mud, fighting for their living, dead and dying mates as much as themselves, were running low on ammunition. A desperate call went out and two RAAF Hueys were loaded up with boxes of 7.62mm cartridges and grenades. Despite ground fire from below, the daring pilots dropped their loads with pinpoint accuracy.

The Company Sergeant Major, Big Jack Kirby, supervised the distribution of ammunition, and with full magazines, morale improved. Even better was news of a relief column on the way, including Armoured Personnel Carriers, but the creeks were rising quickly, and some doubted they would get through.

Finally, however, at around 1900, the relief force reached the battle zone, engaging the enemy and driving them off. D Company had suffered terrible casualties: 18 dead and 24 wounded, the largest Australian loss of life of any single engagement in the Vietnam War. Yet, when mopping-up operations resumed the next morning, the bodies of at least 245 Viet Cong and NVA soldiers were found around the company perimeter.

The Battle of Long Tan was a costly but decisive victory that may have prevented a major attack on the Nui

Dat base. It had lasting implications for peace in Phuoc Tuy Province.

Photo credit: Steve Johns

THE PEOPLE BEHIND THE NAMES

Bennelong

It's hard to think of a born and bred Australian who inspired more place names than Bennelong.

His name lives on at Bennelong Point, where the Opera House now stands; the electorate of Bennelong; and Bennelong Park at Kissing Point. A genus of shrimp, Bennelongia, was also named after him. Some suburbs, streets and locations similar to Bennelong's other traditional name, Woollarawarre, may also owe their origins to this immensely interesting man. The development at Barangaroo is named after his first wife, herself a powerful figure amongst the Cammeraygal people.

Bennelong was a member of the Wangal clan, whose country stretched from Parramatta to Darling Harbour, and included highly productive estuarine hunting grounds. He was abducted from his people on the orders of Governor Arthur Phillip, apparently in an effort to better understand local Indigenous groups. At that time Bennelong was around twenty-five years old, described by a Captain Watkin Tench as being: 'of good statue, and stoutly made, with a bold intrepid countenance, which bespoke defiance and revenge.' The young Bennelong lived in Governor Phillip's home and soon had a working grasp of the English language as well as a taste for food and liquor. He could, apparently, eat a week's rations in a day. Despite this largesse, the bush life called to him and he escaped after a few months. He turned up later at Manly in a confrontation between armed parties that resulted in Phillip being wounded by a spear. Bennelong was so worried about his former host that he took to hanging around the settlement again. By 1791 he lived in a brick hut built for him at Bennelong Point.

Bennelong Point

Barangaroo gave birth to a daughter called Dilboong, but the young mother died soon after. Her body was wrapped in an English blanket, and burned along with a basket of her fishing gear. The service was accompanied by a traditional shower of thrown spears.

Dilboong also died while still an infant, and Bennelong begged Phillip to let him bury her in his garden. He produced only one other confirmed descendant, a boy called Thomas Coke, most likely the son of his second wife. Thomas was raised by a clergyman and died at the age of just twenty.

When Governor Phillip returned to England in late 1792, Bennelong went with him.

According to an account by Royal Navy Lieutenant James Grant:

> *Benelong (sic) visited England with*

> *Governor Philips, and returned to New South Wales with Governor Hunter; and I am sorry to add, far from being improved by the voyage. He has unfortunately acquired a fondness for strong liquors, and is apt to take them to a great excess, at which time he proves very disorderly and ungovernable. He still retains the highest respect for Governor Philips (sic), and discovers a grateful sense of the favours received at his hands.*

On his return, Bennelong found that his second wife had left him, and he spent the rest of his life caught between two worlds. He was an adviser to Governor Hunter, but also an elder of his people, participating fully in ceremonies and payback fights. His two favourite activities, it was said, were 'love and war.'

Bennelong died in January 1813 at Kissing Point, and was buried in an orchard belonging to his friend and early brewer, James Squire. The grave site has recently been located, now under a front yard in the suburb of Putney.

So who the hell was Alice anyway?

William Whitfield Mills, Overseer of Section C of the Overland Telegraph line from Adelaide to Darwin, was heading north with men and heavy equipment, on the way to the starting point for his section of the line. He wrote in a report to his boss, Charles Todd, Superintendent of Telegraphs:

> *On the 7th (March 1871) I started again for the ranges, the drays in the meantime following the Hugh (River).*

> *On March 11th I again arrived at the MacDonnell Ranges and was successful in finding a pass, about 30 miles east of Stuart's track, with numerous waterholes and springs, the principal of which is the Alice Spring which I had the honour of naming after Mrs Todd.*

Lady Alice Todd, wife of the Superintendent of Telegraphs, inspired not only the name of the town, Alice Springs, but also the Todd River. Who was she, and why did she deserve such adoration?

Alice Gillam Bell was born in 1836 in Cambridgeshire, England. When she was twelve years old, Charles Heavitree Todd, assistant Astronomer at the Royal Observatory, Greenwich, came to call on her mother. Alice watched the visitor intently, impressed by his serious ways and dark good looks

'If no one else will have you, then I will marry you, Mr Todd,' she told him.

As their daughter, Lorna, later wrote:

> *In the rather lonely years when my father worked at the Cambridge Observatory — he was too busy for the making of friends — his thoughts, I know, often turned to his first visit to Mrs Edward Bell, and to the little girl of twelve lying on a bear skin rug in front of the fire, who so kindly promised to marry him if nobody else would. That may well be regarded as the raising of the first pole of the Overland Line!*
>
> *Five years later when my father called on Mrs Bell to tell her of the offer he had had of a position in South Australia — a land so far away, and a life so crude and rough, he felt he could hardly ask anyone to come*

> with him and share it — Alice again made history when she said so obligingly, 'I will go with you Mr Todd.'

Unlikely as it must have seemed at the time, the pair exchanged vows and Charles whisked Alice away to Adelaide, Australia. After many years of working on electrical apparatus for the transmission of time signals he had been appointed as the Superintendent of Electric Telegraph by the South Australian Government.

> She was not 18 when they sailed in the good ship 'Irene' under good Capt. Bruce. A ship of 300 tons. It is true that they had two state cabins with their own furniture and my mother had her 'lady's maid,' but think of the dark of that ship with no electric light, and of the heat when they were becalmed in the doldrums for three weeks with no fans to help. Think too of the unsuitability of their clothes — my mother in her many petticoats and her little matron's bonnet tied tightly under chin with broad ribbons and her crinoline which must have taken up so much room in the cabin!
>
> The landing in such unsuitable clothes on a roasting hot day in November, and the drive in a bullock wagon through the sandy scrub from Port Adelaide to Woodville must have sorely tried my mother.
>
> A small house in Angas street had been found for my parents. This house to my mother was an excitement, her own home. It was fun to her, even to having to buy all water for household and

> *drinking purposes from a cart in the street which called daily. I suppose the water came from the Torrens Creek and was carted up in tins.*

Over the years, away from home setting up a link between Adelaide and Melbourne, then the Overland Telegraph to Darwin, Charles wrote to his wife daily. Each letter started out with, 'My Dearest Alice.' He talked of his life in remote places, and his troubles with getting the telegraph lines across some of the most rugged and isolated terrain on earth.

From the Roper River, near a particularly difficult part of the construction, he wrote, 'I wish you could see it, especially at sunset, when the tints and reflections on the water are most beautiful.'

The strength of Charles and Alice's relationship shows through in those letters, feelings growing stronger from the foundations laid all those years earlier in that little home in Cambridgeshire. All who knew Alice loved her, and as her daughter Lorna later wrote:

No one could look into my mother's blue eyes, which always had a twinkle of fun in them, without being sure of her enjoyment of life.

The couple had two sons and four daughters, and were regular churchgoers as well as members of Adelaide society in the latter half of the nineteenth century.

Alice died in 1898 at the age of just 62, when the town she gave her name to was well on its way to becoming a vibrant outback community. Her husband's middle name was used to name Heavitree Gap, now the southern entrance to town. Charles died at Semaphore, Adelaide, of gangrene, in 1910.

'I will marry you, Mr Todd,' Alice said as a twelve year old. But she could surely not have imagined that with those simple words her name would live on as the title of arguably Australia's most iconic outback city.

Paddy Cahill

Originally from the Darling Downs, Paddy Cahill made his name in the Northern Territory as a bushman, stockman and buffalo hunter.

Paddy and his two brothers, Tom and Matt, all cut their teeth with the famous Nat Buchanan on one of Australia's biggest cattle drives, from St George in Queensland to Glencoe Station in the Northern Territory. All three stayed on in the frontier country, Paddy forming Oenpelli Station on the East Alligator River, where he produced beef and even milk from a small dairy herd.

Within a few years, with a burgeoning market for hides, Paddy started buffalo hunting. This was a risky undertaking, pursued in wetlands frequented by huge crocs. The ground was treacherous for horses, and therefore the key to the business was a good supply of surefooted mounts, and a skilful team. Paddy's horse St Lawrence was a legend in the north, and one of the reasons for his success.

The team had to work with precision. Generally Paddy and another man were mounted during the 'run', both armed with Martini Enfield carbines. The early models were chambered in .450 calibre, then later the new .303 military cartridge. The men on horseback would ride in close and shoot at point blank range, while a steady foot shooter could take out running animals. Once the buffalo were down they would be finished off while the skinners stropped their knives and started work.

Paddy Cahill on horseback

Injuries and deaths amongst the men were common, often from being thrown and occasionally from being attacked by a wounded or enraged buffalo. Horses were often gored. It was bloody and dangerous work; not for the fainthearted. Most of the skinners and foot shooters were Aboriginal, who were fearless, and used to the harsh conditions in the tropical Top End.

At the beginning of the season agents in Darwin would offer contracts for whatever number of hides the buffalo hunters thought they could manage, and the product, salted down and tied into bales, would be collected from bush jetties on the East Alligator River, and the King or Liverpool Rivers for the shooters working further east. Paddy Cahill and his team produced at least 1600 hides each year.

Paddy Cahill sold up in 1913, and died of influenza in Sydney ten years later. Next time you throw a lure in at Cahill's Crossing, spare a thought for the man it's named after.

Buckley's Chance

William Buckley was an English bricklayer, and ex-soldier, transported to Australia in 1803 for being caught in possession of stolen goods. He was a huge man, standing six foot six in his socks. Resuming his trade at Port Phillip, he laid the first brick of the town that would eventually become Melbourne.

Escaping with five mates from a work party, one man was shot dead and another recaptured. Two others elected to return to Port Phillip after a week of starving in the bush. Only William Buckley stayed in the wilderness, eating anything he could find to sustain him. Finding a spear protruding from an Indigenous grave site, he put it to good use, much to the amazement of local Aborigines who figured he had to be the reincarnation of the man who had once owned it.

For thirty-two years Buckley lived with the Port Phillip tribes, and when he finally wandered back into the settlement, he'd forgotten how to speak English. Pardoned, but forced to live and work with the whites, he was sickened by their treatment of his Indigenous 'families' and he eventually moved to Hobart. Crowds gathered to get a look at the 'Wild White Man.'

Buckley married at age sixty, and died ten years later after a wagon accident.

The Australian slang term 'Buckley's Chance' came about when he first escaped into the bush as a young man, because no one expected him to survive.

It seems likely that the later addition to this saying, 'Buckley's and None,' came about after the department store, Buckley and Nunn, opened its doors in Melbourne in 1851

LAW MAKERS AND LAW BREAKERS

Making Fools of the Law

There's a long tradition of laughing at authority in Australia. Holding the constabulary up to ridicule was often the response to oppressive police tactics.

Australian bushrangers loved nothing better than making fools of the "traps." Some entered stolen racehorses in bush races and won, or even impersonated the police commanders who were hunting them. Many were such supreme bushmen, that they were able to evade their pursuers for years.

Escaping from custody was a great lark ...

Bushranger Captain Thunderbolt escaped the infamous Cockatoo Island by swimming across a dangerous stretch of water to shore. He remained at large for six years, and showed his contempt for the police by carrying an empty pistol.

Galloping Jones was known for running off from his police escort just for fun, then allowing himself to be recaptured; once he'd had a drink and a feed.

This account from the diary of early Territory policeman, Augustus Lucanus (who was once a soldier in the German army), had a similar theme:

> *Being transferred to Pine Creek and put in charge of the station, I had plenty of riding and bush work to do. My patrol extended to the Katherine River. One day I had to take a white prisoner and hand him on to the next station, to be forwarded to Palmerston. A heavy storm came up.*
>
> *The rain and lightning were terrible. There was one fearful clap of thunder, worse than the rest, after which pieces of timber went flying all ways. A dry tree close by us had been struck. The horses bolted, and by the time I had managed to pull up my frightened mount I could see nothing of my prisoner. I searched and tried to find some tracks, but with no success. The rain had washed them completely out, so I rode on to camp at the Union. Arriving at the hotel I found my prisoner waiting for me in the bar. He was having a whisky. I was very pleased at this.*

Lucanus went on to say that he wouldn't have been so worried if the prisoner was Chinese, for the practice at the time was to simply grab another one, regardless of his innocence.

This true story comes from Woodend in the Macedon Ranges, Victoria, way back in 1902.

A young constable by the name of McKane was trying to arrest an out-of-control drunk outside the local hotel, but the drunk knew how to handle himself and was making things difficult. McKane spied a teenage boy watching and called out.

'Hey you, come and give us a hand instead of standing there gawkin'.'

Taylor did as he was told, and the two of them managed

to drag the man all the way to the lock-up out the back of the police station – a dark cell made of logs with a heavy wood and iron door. It was only a small town so McKane manned the station alone.

Once they had the drunk inside the cell, the constable decided to search him for weapons or money, so he asked Taylor to hold the door open while he did so.

Whether the boy got distracted, or he simply wasn't strong enough to hold the door against a sudden gust of wind, we'll never know.

Either way, the door slammed shut, locking all three of them inside: a policeman, a boy, and a violent drunk.

McKane and Taylor screamed, hammered and cooeed, but the townspeople all knew that a drunk had been arrested so they assumed it was him making all the noise. Sounds of scuffling and yelling went on all night.

The next morning a council worker, heading past on his way to work, went over to investigate and released the unhappy pair. You can only imagine how the people of Woodend must have laughed when the story got out.

As for the drunk – he must have entertained many a bar with tales of his night in the Woodend lock-up.

Tom Turner – Pine Creek Cop

Tom Turner was just nineteen years old when he quit his trade as an iron and wire worker, and joined the South Australian Police Force. Posted to the mining town of Kapunda in 1907, a local girl soon caught his eye. Her name was Pauline Alma Rohde.

Tom started courting the young trainee nurse, but she was no pushover. Tom might have been tall and fit, with a curious outlook and strong character, but Alma (as she was usually known) wanted security.

'We'll wait,' she said, 'until you're settled somewhere.'

Back then the Northern Territory was governed by South Australia, and in 1910 Tom was posted to the remote town of Pine Creek. This was a rough mining town with characters as hard as the country around it, and big problems with grog and opium consumption.

Tom and Alma agreed to become informally engaged as he headed off for the first leg of the journey north. He reached Oodnadatta by train, then travelled by camel train through the Centre. Tom soon found that he loved the outback with a passion, and that he had a talent for remote police work. He roamed far and wide on camel and horse patrols, and kept law and order in 'his' town with a keen eye and iron hand.

He also found time to compete in both cycling and foot races, winning more than a few pounds in prize money. Most of this extra cash, no doubt, went towards his savings for an upcoming honeymoon. He also loved to grow pawpaws, vegetables and mangoes in a plot behind the police station.

Constable Tom Turner in front of Pine Creek Police Station (NT Library)

Preparations for a wedding were well underway when World War One broke out, throwing their plans into disarray. Alma wrote her betrothed a tearful letter, explaining that she felt she had to play her part in the war effort, and that he would have to wait.

The young nurse sailed off to war on the Canberra, serving in India, the Persian Gulf, and in a hospital ship off the coast of France. Her wartime duties must have taken an emotional toll, and Tom would have found it hard to understand how she had changed, despite their constant letters to and from the front lines.

The long engagement stretched on until 1926, when the couple finally married in Adelaide. After nearly twenty years of courtship Alma headed north to share the Pine Creek Police Station with the love of her life. The trip took twenty-five days by motor car.

In 1932 the Great Depression was beginning to bite all across Australia. An army of desperate, unemployed men hit the road. When the Northern Territory government offered a weekly wage of one pound for all comers, in return for a day's work, men started to arrive in their thousands.

But the Government, realising that they'd opened the floodgates for more trouble than they wanted, changed their mind so that only official residents could apply. The result was a surge of anger.

Pine Creek erupted into nothing short of a battleground. The hotel, owned by the Young family, was banned by the mob for cutting off their credit. They then assaulted anyone who tried to drink there. Blood apparently, had to be hosed from the floorboards.

When police reinforcements arrived from Darwin, forty or more unemployed men barricaded themselves in the abandoned hospital and were only ejected by police firing live rounds, ducking bullets from the opposition. After police arrested one of the mob and took him away, the station itself came under attack.

Tom Turner was badly beaten with fists, boots and clubs, and that night an explosive charge was placed under the courthouse. The explosion rocked Tom and Alma's bedroom, and Tom was badly injured, almost losing an eye and spending five weeks in Darwin hospital.

Tom's last Territory posting was to Daly River, where he and Alma cemented themselves as a formidable pair. With Alma's nursing skills, and Tom's penchant for law and order, they took a humanitarian approach, helping preserve the health, pride and welfare of some 3000 local Indigenous people. They stayed on after Darwin was bombed, and did not leave the Territory until 1944 when the crisis was over, and the military took over the police station.

A creek in the Daly River area, Tom Turner's Creek, was named after Tom, and retains that name to this day.

Alma died in 1960, and, broken-hearted, Tom also died just six weeks later. As I delved into this story, I couldn't help thinking that Tom and Alma were really special Australians.

**Horseshoe Creek Police Station, between Pine Creek and Katherine.
Credit: James Pinkerton Campbell**

The Capture of the Kenniff Brothers

It was April the 2nd 1902 when Queensland policeman, Constable Doyle, closed in on Patrick and James Kenniff at a rugged mountain hideout called Lethbridge's Pocket. With the manager of Carnarvon Station, Albert Dahlke, and a tracker called Sam Johnson for company, Doyle stealthily approached the camp.

Wanted for horse stealing, Jim and Patrick had been in trouble with the law before, and both had served time. Born and raised in New South Wales, they moved to Queensland one step ahead of the bailiffs. Then, from a base in the Upper Warrego area they raced horses, ran illegal books, and stole livestock at night. When police arranged for the lease on their land to be terminated, the brothers became outlaws, and rarely rode unarmed.

Dahlke and Constable Doyle got lucky at first. Patrick managed to slip away, but they chased Jim on horseback and rode him down. When tracker Sam Johnson was sent back to fetch handcuffs he heard five gunshots. Patrick had returned for his brother, with deadly result.

Sam was forced to ride for his life, but he returned later with a man called Burke. In two pack bags they found the charred remains of Dahlke and Doyle.

A huge manhunt followed, but the two brothers stayed on the loose for more than two months before they were tracked to a ridge just south of Mitchell called Bottle Tree Hill (pictured below). Four policemen; Constables Tasker, Scanlan, Meston and Cramb surrounded the camp, and waited until sunrise when they were able to surprise the sleeping men. Patrick and Jim both fled on foot.

Patrick had no time to locate a weapon, and was easily ridden down by Constable Cramb. Jim fled with both loaded rifles, but was captured on the road back towards Mitchell, near what is now called Arrest Creek.

The brothers were placed on trial on Brisbane, and found guilty of wilful murder. Public sympathy, however, was on the side of the Kenniff brothers, in part because of a groundswell of anti-establishment feeling at the time. Jim's sentence was commuted to life imprisonment, but Patrick was promised an appointment with the gallows.

Four thousand people marched outside Brisbane's Boggo Road Gaol to protest the execution, but the government held firm. Patrick had his neck broken by the rope on the 12th of January, 1903, still protesting his innocence.

Below are the words to one of several ballads in circulation at the time. They are believed to have greatly boosted public sympathy for Patrick and his brother, who served only twelve years of his life sentence.

THE EXECUTION OF PADDY KENNIFF
by John Creevey 1867-1912

With head erect he left his cell, he needed no man's aid,
He walked upon the scaffold, and this is what he said:
"My name is Patrick Kenniff, I am condemned to die,
As witness of my innocence I call my God on high.
To my few friends I bid farewell, the last farewell I'll say,
My time has come and soon I'll be a lifeless lump of clay.
I wish to thank the warders, who have treated me so well,
And the Rev. Father O'Riley, who saved my soul from hell."
Then forward came the noble priest, and shook poor Paddy's hand,
"Paradise is yours," he said, "when you quit this sinful land."
The good priest then began to pray, he prayed 'till all was o'er,
The lever wrenched the scaffold sprung, poor Paddy was no more;
He may have died an innocent man, 'tis very hard to say,
There were other men in Killman's Gap, upon that fatal day;
Then let's not judge lest we be judged, by him who judges all,
And never despise your fellow man, if he should chance to fall.

Moondyne Joe

Joe Johns, or Moondyne Joe, was a Western Australian bushranger and horse thief. A top-notch bushman, he escaped from prison several times, and used his tracking skills and local knowledge to evade capture over and over again. In 1867, he also pulled off one of the cleverest escapes in Australian history.

Joe was in Fremantle Gaol, confined to a special cell lined with Jarrah sleepers, when the prison doctor warned that he needed exercise or faced serious ill-health. Wary because of Joe's penchant for escaping, the authorities allowed him to break rocks for a couple of hours each day. Unlike the other prisoners, however, they would not let him leave the prison, instead bringing in dray-loads of limestone for him to crush, dumping it just inside the walls.

Day after day, Joe went to work with the sledgehammer, while a warder kept a watchful eye on him from a chair nearby. Slowly the piles of crushed rock grew higher, until the warder could see only Joe's hat. One afternoon, the warder realised that although he could still see the hat, the noise of hammer on rock had stopped.

Walking across to investigate, the warder found Joe's hat on a shovel handle stuck in the ground, and a sizeable hole in the prison wall. Joe was nowhere to be seen. Of course, he had been secretly attacking the wall for days, covering it with loose rock each time.

The Fremantle Correspondent from the Perth Gazette and West Australian Times summed up the mood of the Western Australian public.

> *Probably no event in the colony ever more tickled the risible faculties of the public, than did the escape of the notorious convict 'Moondyne Joe,' on the afternoon of Thursday, last week. Much of the amusement felt arose from remembrance of the theatrical exhibition made of Joe by the Acting Comptroller General, when he was last captured. Chaining him to a post in one of the yards, and Mr Hampton improving the occasion by addressing the assembled prisoners, and pointing out to them Joe's sad condition, as an example of what would befall them if they went and did likewise. Joe's ingenuity in making his escape from his apparently hopeless condition, has gained him many sympathisers.*

They did recapture Moondyne Joe, but it took them two years to do so. Joe died in 1900 from dementia.

Footnote: I was interested to find, during my researches of Elizabeth Woolcock, also the subject of an article in this book, that she was a distant relative of Moondyne Joe.

Harry Readford

Some men are born bad, some become outlaws through persecution and desperation. Some, like Harry Readford, are opportunists, who commit their crimes through a sense of fun and love of a challenge.

Even as a young man, Harry was a unusually tall and impressive figure, face shaded by his hat and protected by a thick, curling beard. He smoked cigars and never seemed to run short of these luxuries. He never said a word without thinking it through first, and was generous and chivalrous to a fault.

Born in Mudgee in 1842, youngest of seven children, Harry knew plenty about living rough. He also had a rare understanding of horses, and took to cattle work like he was born to it. In Western Queensland he found his calling, working on Bowen Downs Station, a property that stretched for well over a hundred miles along the Thomson River.

It was there one day, in a remote stock camp with his mates George and Bill that Harry first started musing about 'all those unsupervised cattle.' Bowen Downs carried some 60 000 head at the time.

'I believe,' Harry said, 'that these damn cattle aren't hardly seen from one year to the next. Why a man could ride off with a bunch of them in September and they might not be missed until June. Perhaps not even then.'

The idea firmed into a plan over the coming weeks. The three men quit their jobs and rode away, returning at night to remote hill country where they built a set of yards and set about secretly mustering Bowen Downs cattle. They were careful to take only cleanskins and to leave behind any stock that might be recognised.

Unfortunately as they finally set off with 1000 head of cattle, a distinctive white bull, a prized possession of the Mt Cornish Outstation, joined up with the mob. Harry and his mates argued over what to do with him while they escorted their stolen cattle down Coopers Creek en route to South Australia.

'Best to shoot that bastard and leave him in a ditch,' Harry said.

But the others disagreed. The bull was worth five hundred pounds and they convinced Harry that they could easily sell the bull to a station owner along the way without the risk of trying to yard him in Adelaide. Harry gave in and they sold the bull to a storekeeper on the remote Strzelecki Creek.

The drive itself was one of the great achievements of Australia's early pastoral history, and this was not lost on the people of Adelaide. Harry, George and Bill found themselves being hailed as trailblazers, leading to some uncomfortable questions about the source of the cattle. When news of the white bull trickled through to Adelaide, trouble was on the way.

Harry was enjoying the proceeds of the sales, staying in private rooms at one of the city's best hotels, when the clerk from the saleyards knocked on the door and asked him for a moment of his time.

'I'm only telling you this because you're such a gentleman and always done right by me. The police are coming for you. Get out of town fast if you can.'

Riding like the born horseman he was, across South Australia, through Victoria and into New South Wales, Harry decided that the best way to throw the police off was to lose himself in some nondescript country town. He was smart enough not to ride openly into his birth place of Mudgee, but found the ideal retreat just a little further north.

The town of Gulgong, in 1871, was rapidly changing from a sleepy hamlet to a set of bare hills swarming with diggers. The rush had started when a man called Tom Saunders found fourteen ounces of gold, and the news went out on the wires and bush telegraph to every corner of the colony. Over the next ten years the Gulgong fields would produce some fifteen tonnes of the precious metal.

With 20 000 hopefuls arriving with their shovels and pans, Gulgong was the perfect place for Harry to hide while the police searched fruitlessly elsewhere. He changed his name and used some of the proceeds from the big cattle theft to buy a hotel.

Soon one of the top businessman in town, Harry began to ride to Mudgee, always after dark, to visit with an old family connection. Her name was Elizabeth Jane Skuthorpe, now a thirty-two-year-old widow.

The fling soon became a fully-fledged love affair. Harry galloping south every second night, sleeping in Elizabeth's arms, then leaving before the break of day. Finally, he selected a diamond studded ring and proposed to Elizabeth on his knees. Unable to risk a public wedding, they married in private, at the Mudgee home of Elizabeth's sister.

Living in the hotel in Gulgong, life was good for the newlyweds. Their daughter Jemima came along in 1872. Harry enjoyed life as a popular hotelier, father and husband. His years as a stockman seemed like a lifetime ago, but the bush has a habit of calling back to its own.

Things didn't stay well for long ...

Harry had an employee at the hotel, an itinerant boy who performed odd jobs around the place. He collected glasses, cleaned rooms, hosed down the pavement and slept in the stables.

After money and valuables started disappearing from around the hotel, Harry was watching the boy carefully.

One evening, when the cash box was found to be missing, the boy and a horse were also gone. It was a grave mistake to try to outdo Harry Readford on a horse.

Harry Readford leaving town by John Morrison

With a couple of hours Harry had caught up with the boy on the Sydney road, still with the cash box. After a short chase the older man knocked the boy from his mount and dragged him back to Gulgong.

The boy went on trial in the courthouse. It was an open and shut case, and Harry was there to see that justice was done. Unfortunately, it just so happened that a Queensland detective was in the courtroom that day. Worse still, he had earlier been assigned to the case of the stolen Bowen Downs cattle.

The detective recognised Readford straight away. He sidled out of the courthouse, heading for the adjacent police station for backup. Within minutes one of the local policemen was whispering in Harry's ear.

'They're coming for you. Get out of here.'

Another timely warning, but this time Harry had a wife and child to consider.

This story of Harry Readford has more twists and turns than an outback trail. The police nabbed him on the road to Sydney, and he was handed, with great fanfare and announcements by senior police, over to the Queensland authorities.

But by then Harry was a folk hero. Every Australian

loved the story of a man bold enough to steal 1000 head of cattle and drove them down a desert track no one had dared to attempt. On trial in Roma, the jury found him not guilty and set him free. He was carried on the shoulders of his mates out of the courtroom.

The judge was furious, and the Queensland justice department so annoyed by Harry's acquittal that Roma's courthouse was shut down for two years!

Yet Harry was a marked man, and couldn't keep himself out of trouble. In the next few years he famously pioneered the use of acid to dissolve any previous brand from a cow's hide, but it was his love of fine horses that brought him undone. He was charged with stealing a horse from Eton Vale, and served fifteen months in Brisbane's Boggo Road Gaol.

From the time of his release Harry lived and worked almost entirely in the bush. He started off droving cattle from the Atherton Tablelands to Dubbo, and then did hundreds of trips across North Queensland and beyond.

Apart from the Bowen Downs cattle theft, however, Harry Readford will be best remembered as the man who first took up Brunette Downs cattle station, on the Barkly Tableland, on behalf of Macdonald, Smith and Company. He arrived from Queensland with 3000 cattle, finding one of Australia's most productive grasslands, horizon to horizon of waving Mitchell grass.

Harry spent much of the rest of his life on Brunette Downs and close by. There was even a waterhole on Corella Creek named after him. After a hard day in the saddle he liked to go there and read bush poetry. Harry managed Macarthur River Station for a time, but in his last couple of years he wandered from station to station, described by a man who knew him as 'a very old, unwanted and forgotten man.'

It's unlikely that Harry had much contact with his wife and daughter, who were living in Sydney by then, many weeks away on horseback. Elizabeth died peacefully in 1925, at Macquarie Park at the ripe old age of 85. Harry was not so fortunate.

There are conflicting reports of his death. One story is

that in March 1901, he attempted to swim his horse across the flooded Corella Creek, was hit by a floating tree trunk and drowned. The other is that one of his favourite horses got tangled in her hobbles in the same creek, and he lost his life trying to untangle her.

Either way, his body was found by a young Aboriginal woman, who wrapped him in his swag and buried him. A sheet of corrugated iron, set in the earth, marked his grave until at least the 1940s. A stone marker with iron barriers was eventually erected.

Harry is remembered as an expert horseman and cattleman, for his mischievous nature and as a true friend to his mates. He became the inspiration for the main character in Rolf Boldrewood's book, 'Robbery Under Arms,' and each year hundreds of Australians gather for the 'Harry Redford Cattle Drive' near Aramac in Queensland.

Collateral Damage

Spare a thought for the Jones family, who owned the Glenrowan Hotel when the Kelly Gang decided to use it as the venue for a battle with police.

Ann Jones was the owner and publican. In the battle her pride and joy was burned to the ground. Her son John was shot and killed in the crossfire. Her daughter Jane also caught a stray bullet, but lingered on for two years before dying from her wounds.

Documents found at the Supreme Court stated, in Ann's own words:

"Brave police! They lay in the gullies, and behind the trees, and shot bullets at the house, knowing that it was full of people. My poor innocent little children suffered most. When my dead little boy was hit he stood up, looked around, and then fell down. 'Oh God,' he cried, in such a piteous voice. 'Mother, dear mother, I'm shot!'"

After the siege, the distraught Ann screamed abuse at the police, and was arrested for being a Kelly sympathiser.

"The police have said things about my character," she said later. "Most of them never had any."

SHIPS, IMMIGRANTS AND PIRATES

Mary Watson of Lizard Island

The ruins of a stone cottage, once the home of pioneer Mary Watson, lie crumbling up behind the beach at Watson's Bay on Lizard Island, three hundred kilometres north of Cairns.

Mary was born in Cornwall, and her family settled in Maryborough, Queensland, when she was seventeen. Both educated and musical, Mary easily won a position in Brisbane as a governess.

Mary's employer, Mr Bouel, decided that her talents were wasted teaching children. He took her to Cooktown to play piano in a hotel he owned there, and in that wild frontier town she grew up fast.

Belting out popular tunes on the piano at the bar, Mary couldn't help but notice when a handsome, fit man called Robert Watson swaggered in one night. Mary learned that he, in partnership with his mate Percy Fuller, ran a beche-de-mer (sea cucumber) fishing operation on Lizard Island.

Seduced, perhaps, by tales of one of the world's most beautiful islands, Mary married Bob a few weeks later, and packed for the journey north.

By 1880, still just twenty years old, Mary was running an island household and a small farm with the help of some Chinese labourers. She kept a record of the trials and triumphs of her life in a journal, which survives to this day.

Within a few months Mary was pregnant, and she returned to Cooktown where she gave birth to her son Thomas. Once she felt confident of her abilities in raising the child she headed back to Lizard Island and the love of her life.

Bob, Percy and another man headed off to a distant island on a fishing trip. They had not noticed a fleet of canoes crossing the thirty-five kilometre stretch of water from the mainland.

The Ruins of Mary's Cottage (Author's Photo)

With most of the white men absent, the local Dingaal people, who had fished and hunted on the island for millennia, attacked. Ah Leong, one of the Chinese workers, was killed, and another seriously wounded.

Mary, her baby Thomas, and the wounded man, Ah Sam, put to sea in a cut-down iron water tank. They drifted in terrible heat for eight days before washing up on an uninhabited island in the Howick Group.

The final entry in Mary's journal reads: 'No water. Nearly dead with thirst.' Their bodies were found three months later, and transported to Cooktown for burial.

Taking their cue from an outraged public, the local constabulary inflicted a terrible revenge on the Dingaal people. A sad end to a heart-wrenching tale.

Assisted Immigration

Assisted immigration was a scheme where the Australian colony of Victoria sent agents to the United Kingdom, drumming up interest in the wide open spaces, sunshine, and opportunities available in this new land. The colony paid for the passage of families and individuals, aiming to boost Victoria's population relative to New South Wales. More people, it was decided, would boost economic growth.

By 1851 assisted immigrants were arriving from British ports, mainly on side-paddle steamers, the journey averaging some five months. Each immigrant cost the colony £14 17s 4d.

Some statistics for the year 1852, when gold had been recently discovered, tell an interesting story:

15 477 assisted immigrants arrived on forty-two ships, landed at Melbourne, Portland and Geelong. The ships averaged 827 tons.

5077 were adult males.

5315 were adult females.

5125 were children.

849 people died on the voyage.

270 living children were born on the voyage.

5319 were from England. 7127 were from Scotland.

3001 were from Ireland.

Just 11.3% of these immigrants were able to read and write. By far the lowest literacy rates were amongst the Roman Catholic Irish.

The majority of men listed their occupation as 'agricultural labourer.' Most would take up land and help forge the strong farming communities of Victoria; generally hard workers fully committed to their families and their new country.

In the same year, 1852, the astonishing number of 79 187 unassisted immigrants arrived in Victoria, the majority of them men heading for the goldfields. Only 9072 of these were female. A large but unknown proportion would leave within a few years.

Barbara of the Kaurareg

The year was 1843, and Barbara Thompson was just thirteen years old. At this tender age she had already emigrated with her family from Scotland to Australia, and was living as the de facto wife of a man called William Thompson. They were both on board the cutter America when it ran into a reef off Possession Island, Cape York.

The boat was breaking up on rocks when a lookout sighted a fleet of canoes heading for the wreck, bristling with spears and war clubs. Attempts to parley with the Kaurareg warriors failed. Every man on board was slaughtered, and the doomed ship ransacked.

When the Kaurareg chief, a man called Peaquee, saw Barbara, she reminded him of his daughter, who had recently died. He ordered that she be spared and taken ashore alive.

For five years Barbara lived the life of the chief's daughter, until a party from a passing ship, the HMS Rattlesnake, came ashore for water. While they were trading with the Kaurareg, they spotted a naked white girl, and after establishing her story, took her aboard and back to civilisation.

Barbara would later marry twice, and became the

subject of Ion Idriess's fictional account: Isles of Despair.

Charlotte Badger

Charlotte Badger was a female convict with sex appeal, irresistible to men and women alike, and Australia's only female pirate. Sentenced to penal servitude in Van Diemen's Land, she and her lover Sarah Barnes plotted to turn the tables on their captors. Too late! Arriving in Sydney, the women were shunted aboard a prison brig with the ominous name of 'Venus.'

On the voyage from New South Wales to Hobart, Charlotte got her hooks into the first mate, John Kelly, convincing him to steal a barrel of rum. When the resulting orgy saw the whole gang thrown in chains, Charlotte and her new lover hatched a plan to release certain male convicts, grab the ship's firearms and take over.

They carried out their plan in the dead of night, fuelled by rum, killing those who resisted in a few bloody minutes. Charlotte's first act, once in control, was to tie the captain to the stocks and give him a taste of the cat o' nine tails, lashing his back into a bloody mess before setting him adrift in a small boat. Just days later she managed to attack, board and pillage yet another vessel, all the supplies being transferred to the Venus.

Sailing to New Zealand's Bay of Islands, the mutineers scuttled the brig and went ashore, where they were welcomed by the Maoris. Sarah scored herself a tribal chief and headed inland, while Charlotte, John and another man settled down in the bay.

This idyllic existence lasted for a few years, until a British man o' war arrived, seizing John and the other male mutineer. Charlotte hid herself in time. The two men were taken back to London and hanged.

According to some reports, Charlotte Badger grew hugely fat from her time with the Maoris, and was last seen boarding the SV Lafayette, bound for America, accompanied by a distinctly Polynesian daughter. The Lafayette's captain, apparently, was infatuated with Charlotte. We can only imagine that she lived out her days travelling on the high seas!

The Ethel Pirates

John A Reddell was the owner of a fleet of pearl luggers operating out of Broome, Western Australia. He personally skippered the supply ship for the fleet, a brig by the name of Ethel, and was known as a hard man who pushed his crews to the limit.

In 1899 he sailed out of Roebuck Bay on the Ethel, bound for Lagrange Bay, 200 kilometres to the south. On board was his son, Jack, a first mate by the name of Taylor, and around ten crew, mostly Filipinos. Trouble had been brewing for a while, and mutiny was afoot.

The captain was standing beside the helmsman when one of the ringleaders, most likely the physically powerful Peter Perez, crept up behind him and buried an axe in the back of his head. The boy Jack met the same fate a few moments later, as did the first mate. Two Japanese divers were also hacked to pieces by the blood-crazed crew, and their bodies thrown overboard.

The new leaders, Perez and his friend Pedro de la Cruz, ordered the brig to turn around, setting a course for Timor, then Ambon. On the voyage north they ordered the killing of anyone they suspected of disloyalty.

Arriving off the coast of Ambon they filled the ships'

boats with valuables and stores from the Ethel, scuttled her, then rowed for the coast. There they set about selling the captain's gold watch and a host of other items. The big-spending strangers soon drew the attention of local authorities.

Pearling Lugger in the Torres Strait (National Library of Australia)

They might have got away with it if the Chinese cook, Pooh Ah Ming, hadn't told the whole story to a local schoolmaster. The story was reported, the mutineers arrested, and a British gunboat arrived to take the six main offenders to Fremantle. One man was acquitted, and the other five sentenced to death. Three of those death sentences, however, were commuted.

The Perth Daily Mail recorded the last moments of Pedro de la Cruz and Peter Perez:

> *The prisoners, who were attended to the last by their spiritual advisers, devoutly invoked the Divine mercy, their last words being, O Padre Mio, O Madre Mia (Oh My Father, Oh My Mother) which was repeated several times in the Spanish language. The hangman pulled the lever, and the next mo-*

ment the murderers of Captain Reddell were dangling lifeless in the pit below.

The Wreck of the Tryal

Most Australians have heard of the Batavia shipwreck, and the subsequent mutiny that led to at least one hundred and fifty passengers being slaughtered by the conspirators in one bloody night. Skeletons and weapons have been dug up for decades on the Abrolhos Islands.

There was an earlier shipwreck, the Tryal, that deserves a place in the national consciousness. The Tryal was an English ship, and her crew were almost certainly the first Englishmen to lay eyes on the Australian continent, one hundred and fifty years before James Cook mapped the East Coast.

On the night of May 24, 1622, the Tryal was sailing up the WA coast, heading for Java. The captain John Brooke had not ordered a topmast lookout. A fatal mistake.

At 11pm the Tryal struck reef at what is now called Tryal Rocks. The captain screamed for the crew to try to tack the vessel away, but it had struck hard in just three fathoms of water. Below decks, water was already rushing in.

The Captain, John Brooke, while allowing a crew of two hundred to fight over the forty or so places in the longboat, commandeered the skiff, and filled it with his son, his friends, and all the silver coins from the ship's hold.

The skiff and the longboat then sailed away, leaving one-hundred-and-thirty-nine men screaming in anguish on the ship watching them go, while a heavy surf pounded it to pieces. Making for an island six miles away, they could have returned for survivors, but instead they opted to sail to Java, leaving all the rest of the crew to die.

Unfortunately Brooke lived to spend his stolen silver. The powers that be believed his lies, and even promoted him to other commands. Years later, however, he was convicted for deliberately running another ship aground, and was sent to prison.

Eventually he was released, but his old crew knew the truth, and I don't imagine that the ghosts of those 139 men gave him much peace.

MINERS, MINERALS, AND THINGS THAT GO BANG

Gold Rush on the Palmer River

If you wanted to cook up a wild adventure story, start with a Queensland river blessed with rich alluvial gold. Throw in a bunch of self-reliant prospectors, an uncontrolled stream of Chinese diggers, Martini-Henry rifles, spirited horses, and a tough indigenous nation that resented and fought the intrusion. Throw it all in a pressure-cooker of Cape York heat, and you've got the Palmer River Gold Rush.

In 1872, two brothers from Victoria, William and Frank Hann, along with a botanist, a geologist and others travelled north on a Queensland Government sponsored expedition to investigate the country 'North to the 14th Parallel'. Rugged country even now, in those days Cape York was an area even the toughest settlers and adventurers avoided.

Hann's party located a river beginning in the hills west of Port Douglas, flowing westwards for six-hundred kilometres before it emptied into the Mitchell River, ultimately reaching the Gulf of Carpentaria. He named this waterway the Palmer River after the Chief Secretary of Queensland, Arthur Palmer. Hann and his comrades were the first to pan gold from the river in 1872. The amounts were not significant, but enough to excite some interest back in civilization.

The lure of a brand-new find attracted James Mulligan, a tough Irishman scraping a living on the Etheridge fields, but dreaming of better things. Staking everything on the venture, he outfitted an expedition with five solid mates and rode north into the wilderness.

Goldfields hotel, 1870s. Courtesy State Library of Queensland.

They returned to Georgetown, on the Etheridge fields, after weeks of panning the Palmer River gravels. It was September 1873, when the Mine Warden posted a notice on the walls of his hut: 'JV Mulligan reports the discovery of payable gold on the Palmer River. Those interested may inspect at this office the 102 ounces he has brought back.'

Within a few days, just about every miner in the worked-out Etheridge field had started on the five-hundred-kilometre trek north. Prospectors knew that getting in early on a rush was the key. Some rode horses or perched on a wagon box. Others walked. Many pushed barrows loaded with all their tools and possessions.

Word went out by ship, telegram, word-of-mouth and mail. News reached Brisbane, Sydney, Melbourne, then

Shanghai and San Francisco. The rush was on.

With the wet season not far away, authorities warned of fever, flooded rivers and trouble. Even Mulligan himself wrote to the Queenslander newspaper: 'I do wish to stop this before it grows any more. Already exaggerated accounts and too much excitement exist here. If people rush the place without rations they must perish.'

Yet nothing dimmed the excitement, and when the Government opened a landing on the Endeavour River the gold-seekers poured in by boat as well.

From beginning to end, the Palmer River yielded a fantastic amount of gold. One hundred tons was the official count, but much more was taken away by the Chinese (gold prices were better in China) or carried home by diggers. It was a genuine El Dorado, but harsh beyond belief, and wild by any standards.

The local Merkin people were not nomadic by nature, living in villages of bark-lined huts on the ridges near good hunting and fishing grounds. They went from living in a relatively unspoiled domain, to a hell-hole of shafts, camps, mullock heaps and fires. Trees fell to the axe, waterholes were muddied, and white men and their guns were everywhere. Some shot blacks on sight, and the strong, able spearmen retaliated.

A letter dated October 5, 1873 from an early arrival stated: 'At present the blacks are very bad. It is war to the knife between the whites and them.'

Unsuccessful diggers, handy with their weapons, hired themselves out as bodyguards, standing sentry with their Martini-Henry or Snider rifles, watching for Merkin raiders. Two such characters were 'Sam the Tracker' and Jack Martin, better known as 'The Orphan.' Bored of earning a pittance standing guard for a party of Chinese diggers, the pair instead murdered and robbed the Chinese gold courier headed for Cooktown on his weekly run. With the law on their trail, the pair doubled back and stole seven of the pursuing police horses.

'The Orphan' was later noted for causing trouble, including cattle stealing, in the Gulf, but was never arrested for the Palmer River crimes. In Borroloola, during a drunken fight, he accidentally shot off his own thumb and forefinger.

The town of Palmerville slowly took shape with two stores. Stock was at a premium in the early days, however, and commodities like flour and beef sold out almost as soon as it arrived. The first pubs were basic affairs, little more than bark sheds, filled to capacity with brawling miners and echoing with arguments over territory, for there was no mine warden in the early days. The miners were prospecting for themselves in a free-for-all, centred mainly on the river itself. Gold lying in shallow depressions in the rapids could often be collected by hand. Exclusive territory came only through the use of fists, knives, and revolvers.

As the mining frenzy moved upstream, a new administrative and service centre was formed. This prosperous little settlement was called Maytown. The numbers of Chinese on the fields also exploded. In 1877 the population of the more important settlements was reported by Warden Selheim as follows:

> *Maytown, 900 Europeans and 800 Chinese.*
>
> *Palmerville, 12 Europeans and 600 Chinese.*
>
> *Jessop's, 6 Europeans and 1000 Chinese.*
>
> *Stony Creek, 16 Europeans and 1200 Chinese.*
>
> *Byerstown, 16 Europeans and 800 Chinese.*

The large numbers of Chinese compared to Europeans was a feature of the fields. They kept to themselves, to a large degree, often re-working areas that the whites had already picked over. They built their own little Chinatowns, with joss houses and opium dens in narrow alleys amid mullock heaps.

The Chinese presence on the fields was not all incense and opium, however. At one stage, the Pekinese and Cantonese elements turned on each other in a frenzied battle that lasted for several days. It culminated in the building of a fort by miners from Macao, who moved in on disputed ground while the others were busy fighting.

With the fort under siege by up to 2000 Chinese miners, hundreds were wounded or killed, and only a determined troop of police stopped the fighting. Thirty ringleaders were arrested and charged, while the fight, known as the Battle of Lukinville, was largely ignored by the Australian public and later historians.

Despite the relatively small number of white miners remaining on the fields as the rush went on, the area continued to produce brash, larger than life characters.

The Palmer River was the birthplace of 'Australia's Annie Oakley,' Claudie Lakeland. Claudie's father Billy was a goldfields character famous for battling both black and white, and prospecting deep into the wilds of Cape York where few other gold-seekers dared to go. Claudie grew up on horseback, and with a gun in her hand.

Her fame as a dead-shot grew, and as a young teen she was challenged to, and won, a shooting contest against the policeman from Coen, Roly Garraway. One of her tricks was shooting, with a rifle, pennies thrown into the air.

The notorious 'Maori' Jack Reid and his wife Henrietta operated a store on the fields. Reid had crewed on a notorious blackbirder, the brigantine Carl in the South Pacific waters. This murderous career culminated with the slaughter of sixty captives when the crew saw a British destroyer approaching. The Carl's officers, first mate and some other seamen were charged, though all had their death sentences commuted to life imprisonment. 'Maori' Reid escaped these unpleasant consequences and enjoyed life in the wilder parts of Australia for many years, before dying alone in a hut near Pine Creek, NT, in the 1930s.

While reflecting on the adventurous characters who answered the call of gold, the saddest aspect of this gold rush was how it tore both a river system and the Merkin people apart. For the survivors and the landscape itself, nothing would ever be the same.

Gold was a terrible lure, and in reality, only a few diggers got rich in a life-changing way. For many, prospecting became a way of life, listening for the next whispered talk of a 'find' in some distant and remote location; time to pack the saddle bags and head off, always in the hope of that elusive fortune.

The Big Australian

When boundary rider Charles Rasp stumbled on an interesting hill in far western NSW, with a fractured body of ore running right through it, he wasn't sure if he'd found something of value or not. He consulted his battered copy of 'The Prospector's Guide' to be certain. Within a few weeks he and six others had formed a company called the Barrier Ranges Mining Association, and pegged out six claims.

The partnership included two dam-builders; David James and James Poole, station owner Charles McCullough, head stockman Charles Urquhart, bookkeeper Charles Lind, and jackaroo Philip Charlie.

Rasp and the others thought they'd found a reasonable prospect for tin mining, but things didn't go well at first. The first ore samples they mined and sent away for analysis showed only traces of tin. Conditions were harsh, and necessities like water difficult to obtain.

'At the start it was very bad,' Charles Rasp later told the Melbourne Argus. 'There was no accommodation, water and provisions were scarce and the weather was very trying ... for 12 months it was really doubtful whether we would make anything out of it.'

Lind sold his share for next to nothing. James Poole

swapped his share with Sir Sidney Kidman, for ten cows. Charles Urquhart sold his share back to Charles Rasp for £20.

We can only imagine how much Lind, Urquhart and Poole regretted their rash disposal of the shares. Assays from the next lot of ore samples came back from Adelaide with exciting news. Silver! Some of the richest ore ever seen. All of a sudden the partnership of seven was one of the most talked about companies in the country. It was time for a name change: The Broken Hill Proprietary Company floated on the stock exchange in 1885.

Charles Rasp's hill would go on to be the richest find of silver, lead, and zinc in the history of the world. The share Charles Urquhart sold for £20 in 1884 was worth one million pounds just six years later. In 2017 a one seventh share of BHP Billiton would be worth a staggering twenty billion dollars.

As for Charles Rasp, he married a waitress, and moved to Adelaide. He didn't have too much time to enjoy his wealth, as he died relatively young, at the age of sixty.

Still, few people have made such a contribution to the development of Australia as did Charles Rasp.

The Opalton Heist

At least two bush storytellers have told this yarn from the opal fields. Bruce Simpson says that his story, set in Opalton, is true, and that Ion Idriess heard about it, borrowed it, and moved it to Lightning Ridge. Sounds fair enough to me.

The story goes that two German brothers arrived in Opalton to make their fortunes. After buying their way in they spent months sinking a shaft 25 metres down through hard rock and clay, breaking their hearts and bodies in the process. Finding nothing apart from a few opal chips worth a shilling or two, the brothers chucked in the mining game and left town.

Curiosity got the better of a couple of local gougers called Shillington and Johnson, who went down the shaft for a look. On the way back up they 'knocked off the end of a stone protruding from the wall of the shaft and discovered it was part of an opalised tree containing gem quality opal.'

Breaking up the tree and packing the pieces into a wooden beer case, the two men couldn't believe their luck – this was a once-in-a-lifetime find worth tens of thousands of pounds. Panicking, for they were now a target for thieves all over the opal fields, Shillington and Johnson approached the local police station to help with security. As it happened, the town cop was away, but had left the keys to the lock-up with a local publican.

The fortune in opals was locked securely in a jail cell, and the two lucky men celebrated the night away.

In the morning, however, the beer case full of opals was gone. Police searched the camps, abandoned shafts, and every nook and cranny of the pub, but that incredible treasure was never found.

So that beer case might just be out there somewhere – hidden and forgotten – worth millions of dollars on today's gem market. No one knows if the German brothers ever heard about the treasure they left behind in that mine shaft, and the trouble that followed.

Territory Gold

Back Row (left to right)—William McMinn, John Lewis.
Front Row—Alex. McKay, A. Peachey, Gilbert McMinn
(N.T. 1873).

On January 18, 1872, John Lewis, his brother James, Walter Soward, and a man called Petersen, set off from Adelaide, bound for the Coburg Peninsula, Northern Territory.

There may have been a sore head or two in that party, for there had been a loud farewell lunch the previous day at the Criterion Hotel on King William Street. The trip didn't start well, for John had left their plant at a depot at Gum Creek.

Arriving at the depot John found that an enterprising local had hidden all the horses and demanded a 'reward' of £2 to 'find' them. But John Lewis was not one to be crossed. As he later wrote:

> I gave him the reward, and something into the bargain.

John was that rare type — hardworking, loyal and trustworthy — yet he expected the same qualities in others, and reacted strongly when disappointed.

Born in Brighton, South Australia, in 1844, he grew up roaming the sand hills and beaches. It was there that he first encountered Aborigines, the beginning of a life-long regard for Australia's first people. In a minority amongst his contemporaries, he treated all he encountered with respect.

> *One of my favourite pursuits was, when I got out of school, in very rough weather, to go and lie in the sand hummocks and listen to the breakers rolling in. Another thing I liked was to get into the blacks' camp, and watch them making baskets and mats out of the rushes growing near the beach, and to see them cooking the fish which they secured, and eating what we call the native apple (mundo), which grew in a little bush along the sand hills. I was always very interested in watching what the aborigines did, because I thought they were such wonderful people.*

John ran away from home when he was fourteen, worked on farms for a while, then was an apprentice blacksmith. The bush called him, however, and most of his youth was spent working cattle and sheep. The summons to the Territory had caught him by surprise, when a friend arranged for him to be granted a large parcel of land on the Coburg Peninsula, site of a small and precarious settlement.

It must have seemed like a tall order, to cross the forbidding interior for some land he had never seen, but John was an adventurous soul, and never shy of a challenge.

Finally, at Gum Creek, united with their horses, the small group started north. They were exceptionally well provisioned, with pack saddles made by Henry Dawson in the Burra. The broken horses they rode were good quality, others were quickly taught to tolerate carrying heavy packs.

At first the travellers headed north over terrain they knew well, stopping at stations for respite and company. Locust plagues, however, were roaming South Australia's grasslands, denuding the land of every blade of grass. Stunned at the damage, John and his party skirted east of Lake Torrens and through Leigh Creek, into the Flinders Ranges.

From there, bearing to the North East they reached Mount Lyndhurst, where the grasshoppers numbered 'in the millions.'

> *A swarm came over, cleared all the vegetation out, and drove our horses away.*

To make matters worse, flies were also in plague numbers, and at night mosquitoes would have given them no peace except for the good quality nets they had brought along on the trip.

In between Lake Eyre and Lake Phibbs the locust plague reached its peak.

> *The locusts kept thumping into the faces, noses and eyes of the horses, and they wouldn't face them ... (the locusts) passed through this narrow neck of land in millions, clearing everything before them.*

At Loddon Spa they met a man called Mr Woods, who had been surveying the Telegraph line. Woods gave them a list of waterholes on their route as far north as Charlotte Waters. There was, however, little need for this preparation, for unlike so many earlier whites to travel through Central Australia, John Lewis's party happened to strike one of the best seasons in years. They found good pasture for their horses almost everywhere. Waterholes were brimming full and alive with fish. Even the normally dry Finke River was flowing, and Lewis described it as the best river north of Adelaide.

There were also people at regular intervals, bullockies carting poles for the Overland Telegraph Line, others droving sheep or cattle to feed the crews, and lone prospectors desperate to find that secret reef. Lewis reported contact with numerous Aboriginal people, who he described as 'friendly and harmless,' though pilfering of stores was apparently a problem.

They stopped at the newly built Alice Springs Telegraph Station, and spent time with some of the crews. A job offer from the Telegraph Company meant a chance to earn some cash and get to know the country.

Overland Telegraph Camp (NT Library)

At that time, with the line still incomplete, the telegraph line penetrated from Adelaide north as far as Tennant's Creek, and from Darwin south as far as Daly Waters. In between was a three hundred mile gap. In order to get messages through, John was hired as a pony express, taking telegrams between the two terminus stations, to be retransmitted at the other end. John's employer, Mr Charles Todd (See 'So who the Hell was Alice Anyway?'), apparently referred to the service as an 'Estafette.'

During this time of running messages between the ends of the line, John and his men heard the first news of gold discoveries around Pine Creek. The idea of Territory Gold started to feature in John Lewis's plans. With hundreds of hours of riding, or tramping beside a wagon to think, John put his mind to how much capital he might have at his disposal, and how it could best be deployed in the mining industry.

Finally, the last stage of the Telegraph Line was completed, a momentous occasion:

> *I went with Patterson and Mitchell to a point a few miles east of Frew's*

> Ironstone Ponds, where the two ends of the wire were to be joined, connecting Adelaide with Port Darwin. We met with Harvey, who told us that the wires would not be joined until twelve o'clock; so we returned to the camp, then made for the last join, and arrived there at about twelve o'clock. At ten minutes past twelve on August 22, 1872, the wires were really joined. Twenty one shots were fired from our revolvers, and a bottle of supposed brandy was broken over the last post. (I think it was tea.) Among those present were Messrs Patterson, Rutt, Mitchell, Howley, Ricks, Hands, Bayfield, Hack, and myself. It had long been a desire of mine to see the wire connected between south and north, and I was glad I had seen this accomplished.

The 'Estafette' now redundant, John was free to head north towards the diggings. In September, the Lewis party arrived at Pine Creek. It was at the newer workings twenty five miles away, at Yam Creek, however, where John saw his first glint of the yellow metal.

The Yam Creek goldfield was described in a newspaper report of the day:

> Yam Creek occupies a somewhat prominent position amongst the rising goldfields of the Northern Territory. About 120 miles distant from Port Darwin it is contiguous to, and bears the same name as, one of the stations on the telegraph line. The locality is described as hilly; the rises are steep, rough, and covered with quartz. From all accounts Yam Creek bids fair to distinguish itself amongst reefing districts. The gold is mainly to be found

in the lesser reefs, leaders and spurs which streak the surface of the hill.

John introduced himself to the Mine Warden and the resident trooper, then took a tour to study the workings. One of the miners took him down a shaft to see the reef, winding its way through the parent rock like a snake, with visible gold in the quartz.

Staying for a few days at the Warden's camp, meeting people and studying the ground, John then forged on towards Port Darwin. On the way he encountered groups of miners heading both to and from the diggings. The most unusual of these was eighteen men hauling a heavily-laden bullock dray, lacking the animals to do the work for them.

Also on the way to Port Darwin, a timid Aboriginal man came into the camp, and knowing a few words of English agreed to guide and help them. John christened the newcomer Neddie, and the two would go on to have a long and mutually beneficial relationship.

In Port Darwin there was something of a crisis – three hundred hungry diggers, who had sailed in from all around the globe after hearing of the gold rush, but were dismayed by the heat, costs, and remoteness of mining in Northern Australia. Many hadn't even made it to the diggings themselves, but wanted to get out and had nothing to eat.

They formed an angry mob, threatening to ransack the town. The Police Commissioner, Paul Foelsche, promised them subsistence rations until the next steamer called, defusing the situation.

John started putting his plans into action. Via telegram, he let it be known back in Adelaide that he was in the north and prepared to act for certain business interests.

His first job, however, came through his old employers from the telegraph line. John was asked to provision and man a mining crew, funded by a new concern named the Telegraph Prospecting and Gold Mining Company. John was shrewd enough to take a share for himself.

Within a few days, with a newly purchased dray, forty horses and men, he was on his way back to Yam Creek. One of the men grew sick on the way, and died of apoplexy, but they got the dray and packhorses through, many of which carried stores for other miners, at a premium rate of £60 per ton.

News of new strikes at the 'Howley,' a few miles away saw John and his men investigate the area, but as he said:

> I went several days with a party prospecting in the neighbourhood of the Howley, but we were unsuccessful. Our horses were losing their hair in the wet season; in fact, some of them were quite destitute of hair, and were breaking out in scabs all over the body. The marsh flies were very bad, and we had to make fires all round the camp so that the horses might stand in the smoke to get rid of the flies. The men were still prospecting; but, although gold could be found in many places, there was nothing very profitable.

Meanwhile, however, two men that John had employed for the new company, McGrath and Williams, had pegged some likely looking claims at Pine Creek. The story goes that McGrath, an Irishman, was sitting on a boulder of quartz, despondent after weeks of chipping, crushing and panning.

'Now if only I'd find gold in this damn stone I'm sitting on everything will be alright,' he said.

He apparently looked down, and saw raw gold glinting in the sun. The men hurriedly pegged two claims and sent for John, who came at a gallop.

John named this new find the 'Eleanor Reef' after his sister. They started work on the claims, bringing high-yielding ore out while others scrambled to peg a piece of the action.

Jealous locals, assisted by a corrupt trooper, tried to contest the claims on the basis that they had been incorrectly pegged. The Mining Warden at first dismissed the complaint, but then, on appeal in Darwin, supported it. Faced with losing the claim, John fought a rear-guard court action that finally returned the claims to his company.

Smith, the man who had brought the action, sidled up to John after the court case. 'The property is ours,' he said, 'and if we cannot get it by law we'll get it in some other way.'

John lifted his waistcoat and showed the butt of his revolver, assuring the other man that he and his men were prepared to protect the claims with deadly force, if necessary.

Despite this warning, two weeks later John was half way to Pine Creek when he heard that a party of men were intending to jump the claims the next day, still on the basis that they were incorrectly pegged. Riding swiftly in the darkness, John arrived in the small hours, waking his workers and setting them to the tasks of cutting new pegs and driving them in, as well as building the prescribed trench that needed to surround each claim.

At dawn, when the claim jumpers arrived, they found not only the claims pegged out to the letter of the law, but John and his men, all armed, waiting for them. The attempt failed, and there were no more problems with claim-jumpers.

John was a tireless worker and a consummate planner. He made the river landing called Southport, which was closer to Pine Creek than Port Darwin was, his base. Within a few months, with money flowing from the mines, he had six horse teams supplying the diggings. He built and stocked a bulk-goods warehouse at Southport, filled with goods replenished by a constant flow of vessels, both steam and sail.

The Telegraph Prospecting and Gold Mining Company had invested in a steam powered crushing mill, or battery. John built a substantial jetty at Southport and used it to help with unloading the mass of machinery, before loading it up for the journey to the company mines at Pine Creek.

On the way the drivers discovered that they were carrying casks of rum. They made straws out of bamboo and took turns sucking out the spirit along the way. One team of men were so drunk they lost all their horses overnight, and others became argumentative.

> *One of the men from the camp was abusive. He was called 'Captain' White, and I think he had been imbibing rum freely, as he came up to me in a fighting attitude and was going to dress me down. I had to oblige him. He was very civil afterwards.*

Finally the battery arrived at Pine Creek, and was the first mining machinery to be erected in the Northern Territory. It was soon crushing tons of ore from the shafts, but the results were disappointing, bearing far less than early assays promised. The investors were unhappy, and the funds dried up. John had been forced to pay expenses out of his own pocket. After making his displeasure known, he quit the company, unhappy with his treatment.

By then, however, John had his fingers in so many pies it's a wonder he found time for sleep. As well as his warehousing and carting businesses, he was the manager of more than a dozen different mines, he had the mail run from Southport to Pine Creek, and his steam launches were plying the Blackmore River to Port Darwin and back.

Still, he found time for a quick voyage back to Adelaide on the Tararua. During the trip there was not only a near mutiny, but a fire broke out on board, burning perilously close to a half ton of gunpowder in the holds, the explosion of which would have blown the ship apart. After six weeks at home, organising some investments and sources of capital, John went north to his growing empire.

Again John funded prospectors and sent them out into likely areas. Two of these, Cooper and Auburn, struck good gold at the Howley. The reef became known as the Cosmopolitan, and John's reef was right at the centre. He was offered £5000 for it the same day. He refused.

John's knowledge of the mines was such that a leak appeared in the telegraph service south. Whenever John wired his agents in Adelaide, Philip Levi and Sons, to sell or buy a particular stock, the instruction was whispered to unknown ears. Dozens of other investors immediately tried to do the same, affecting prices adversely and capping John's profits.

Knowing this, while in Adelaide John had arranged with his broker that from then on, if he added the word 'please' it meant that he wanted the broker to do the opposite to the instruction. In other words, 'please buy' meant 'please sell.'

One day, however, the broker was out, leaving his brother, not privy to the ruse, in charge. When John wired through, 'Please buy all available shares in Neate's Goldmining at par', the broker took his words literally.

What this meant was that, after a session of extremely heavy buying, with local investors in a lather trying to get their hands on the Neate's shares at any price, the senior partner came in, saw what had happened, and immediately started selling. The mistake meant that prices were far higher than they would have been otherwise and John made a pile of cash.

While John prospered, he still took losses. The Cosmopolitan reef petered out at depth, and he rued the day he refused the £5000 cash. Men came and went at a rapid rate, and it was hard to keep good workers. The Northern Territory goldfields were a tough proving ground.

> There was a great deal of sickness on the Northern Territory mining fields at about this time, and the living was anything but good; plenty of bully meat and tinned fish of various sorts, weevilly flour and rice, but no fresh meat and very little vegetable food.
>
> Men were suffering a great deal from scurvy, and many were down with jungle and intermittent fever. Every camp along the road had its burying ground, and scarcely a day passed without one or two being buried at the respective camps. Graves were dug, and the poor fellows rolled up in their blankets and placed in the ground. At most of the camps there would be a prayer book, and the burial service would be read, and the death reported to the police.

But still the finds went on. The fabulous Union Reef was discovered by a cartel of Queenslanders, and John describes how the reef ran along the top of a ridge, with visible gold, sparkling in the sunlight, visible from sixty or seventy yards away. He bought a one-sixth share in the mine for £1000 and for six months it paid big money.

Somehow John never let his business interests tie him down. An influx of Chinese workers from Singapore lowered wages bills and saw many previously unprofitable mines restarted. From that time on European miners were in the minority in Pine and Yam Creeks.

When two experienced African explorers went missing in Arnhem Land, John volunteered to lead the rescue party. An adventure into the wilds followed, John in his element, finally penetrating through to Coburg Peninsula without any sign of the explorers, though local Aborigines said that they had been killed.

Inspired by this new area – the original reason for his journey to the Territory – John took out a new lease of some pastoral land on Coburg and proposed to develop it into a Buffalo Station. He set out with a new expedition, but this time found the original inhabitants determined to block his passage. This is one of the few times John Lewis documents shooting at, wounding, and probably killing Aboriginal people. He was far less inclined to resort to weapons than most of his contemporaries, but he was also a determined man, also capable of using violence on his white subordinates and peers when the need arose.

The party reached Coburg, and the men set to work building yards and catching wild buffalo. The place was just too remote to be a success, and eventually John had no choice but to abandon it. His luck in the Northern Territory appeared to have run out. The gold mining frenzy had moved on to Hall's Creek and other places, and there had been a huge drop in the Territory population, making business difficult.

In 1876, John returned to South Australia, living in Burra and working as a Stock and Station Agent for a firm called Liston and Shakes. He married Martha Anne Brooke the same year and the couple had eighteen happy years before she died in 1894.

John still dabbled in mining from time to time, and was at one stage offered a one-fourteenth share in the fledgling Broken Hill mine for £40, of almost incalculable value today. He missed out on the big mine, but speculated in other ventures and made a small fortune.

Entering politics, he became a member of the Legislative Council for the huge Northeast District. In 1906 he moved to Adelaide and purchased a mansion called Benacre. He remarried a year later. John went on to became one of South Australia's most respected statesmen, and his memoirs, Fought and Won, are a remarkable record of his remarkable life.

It was 1909 before John returned to the Territory. He was taking a world tour with his daughters on the steamer, Empire.

> *It quite reminded me of old times when I saw Coburg Peninsula again, with the two prominent hills, Mount Bedwell and Mount Roe, on the left, and Melville Island on the right. We steamed through the Vernons and on to Port Darwin. The Government Resident (Mr Justice Herbert) sent his orderly down with a note inviting me ashore, and offering to lend me a pair of horses to drive round the settlement. My daughters availed themselves of the opportunity of being driven round; and my old friend, Inspector Foelsche, took charge of me. I saw a few of my old friends, among others Mr P. V. Brown, whom I knew at Brighton in the early fifties. I also saw Mrs Ryan, who was in the Territory in the early days, and Mrs Finniss, wife of the late Fred Finniss. Port Darwin has altered somewhat since 1876, but not to the extent that one would expect, considering the advantages it has in its geographical position and the many rich spots of fertile soil. Time would not permit my going out to see the Government Garden, which I understand now is quite a show place. After sending a few telegrams to South Australia and paying my respects to the Government Resident, we were on board by four o'clock, and a few minutes afterwards steamed out of the harbour. I enjoyed the few hours' stay at Port Darwin very much.*

There is always a wistful sadness to a man when he revisits the fields of his youth, back when his ambition and energy were boundless. And for John Lewis it must have been strange to walk that ground again, where once he had been part of the rush for Territory Gold.

The Loaded Dog

Fishing with dynamite was common practice in Australia in years gone by. A farmer near Dorrigo, New South Wales told me about his father blowing up fishing holes in the Nymboida River, backing up a dray and filling it with huge dead Eastern cod and using them for pig feed.

An old local near Kempsey told me about a dynamite fishing trip on the Macleay River in which his mate fused and lit the explosive, but when he tried to throw it into the river it snagged in a tree just in front of them. The two men looked at each other, then set a new Australian record for a hundred-yard dash.

The following newspaper report, telling the story of a dog making off with a lighted stick of dynamite, is from the Walcha News and Southern New England Advocate, 2 March 1907.

The story bears a striking similarity to that told by Henry Lawson in his short story, The Loaded Dog, yet that piece was published six years earlier, in 1901.

Life imitating art?

A Dog with Dynamite.

Two fishermen of Condobolin, New South Wales, had a particularly anxious time a few days ago when trying to catch fish in the Lachlan River. After trying without success in the ordinary way they decided to use dynamite instead. They accordingly charged a bottle with that explosive, then corked it and inserted a fuse through the cork and, applying a match, threw the live explosive into the likely looking hole selected for their great haul. A dog, trained to retrieve, instantly sprang into the water after it, and was soon swimming back with the bottle gripped between his teeth towards his masters. They shouted and stormed at him, but the faithful animal reached the brink, and they ran for their lives, with, of course, the dog with the fatal bottle in his teeth after them. Then followed the dreaded catastrophe. There was a loud and terrific explosion, and when the two dazed men had assured themselves that they were still alive, they looked for the dog. The poor brute had literally been blown to pieces, and practically nothing remained but the retriever's tail.

VICTIMS OF SOCIETY

Elizabeth Woolcock

Thomas Woolcock, Elizabeth, and Thomas Junior. State Library of South Australia.

The Old Adelaide Gaol stands on the south bank of the River Torrens, massive and silent. The thick stone walls, guard towers and block-like cells leave visitors in no doubt that from 1841 to 1988, this was a prison designed to dehumanise and isolate its inhabitants; those that the justice system had decided, for their crimes, to remove from society.

It was here, in the year 1873, that Elizabeth Lillian Woolcock was given just twenty-six days to live. Twenty-six days to ponder her sins. Twenty-six days to imagine how the rope would feel around her neck, and to reflect on the life and eventual crime that had made her a household name – the talk of every household in the state.

Elizabeth was born in Burra, South Australia, in April, 1848, to Cornish parents, John and Elizabeth Oliver. Like many of his countrymen, John had mining in his blood, and the family enjoyed the camaraderie of a strong community, tapping rich copper reefs in the dry hills around the town.

Like many others, the Olivers lived in a home burrowed into the banks of Kooringa Creek. In June 1851, a major flood swept down the waterway, sending a churning wave of destructive water through these underground abodes. At least one man was drowned trying to retrieve his belongings, and it's likely that the Oliver family lost everything they owned. These were tough times, and neither of Elizabeth's younger siblings, John and Catherine, survived early childhood.

When Elizabeth was five years old, her mother left home. John, living at least temporarily at Tynte Street, North Adelaide, placed the following advertisement in the South Australian Register: *This is to certify that my wife, Elizabeth Oliver, has left her home without any just cause or provocation. I will not be accountable for any debts she may incur or contract after this date.*

Unable to stay away from the mining way of life for long, John followed thousands of other gold seekers across the border to Ballarat, hunting the yellow metal while trying to care for his little girl. He staked a claim at Creswick Creek, and Elizabeth was often left in the tent alone when he went out to work, though she was likely to have attended the local school after it opened in 1854.

It was a difficult time. Elizabeth was still a child when the Eureka Rebellion swept through the area. John Oliver played at least a minor role. It seems likely that his daughter was a witness to at least some of the violence that erupted between the diggers and police.

When Elizabeth was seven, she was alone in the tent when an itinerant by the name of George Shawshaw came to the flap and asked for a smoke. Elizabeth gave him her father's pipe, and when he had finished smoking he seized her by the throat, half suffocating her. He then raped her, a crime so vicious that the judge called it 'one of the most atrocious cases' he had ever presided over. Shawshaw was sentenced to death by hanging, though this was commuted to a long jail term.

Elizabeth's injuries were so severe they left her unable to bear children. A local doctor gave her opium for the pain, the beginning of a lifelong addiction, and more changes were on the way. While still a girl she was engaged as a servant to a Mr Lees, a Creswick chemist. Through her early teens Elizabeth had a steady supply of the drug she craved. At fifteen she left her employment and moved to Ballarat, living in a boarding house that may have doubled as a brothel. She was using opium and supplying it to prostitutes, a trade in which she may have been employed herself.

Elizabeth's mother, during this period, had remarried. A few years later, despite facing bankruptcy in 1862, the elder Elizabeth started looking for the daughter she had abandoned so many years earlier.

After receiving a message from a travelling minister, in 1864 Elizabeth moved in with her mother and stepfather at another Cornish mining stronghold in South Australia, Moonta. At this point, for a while at least, the young woman had something of a normal life. Her mother and stepfather were active in the Wesleyan Church, and Elizabeth became a Sunday school teacher. She also took up employment as a servant to a local widower, Thomas Woolcock.

When Elizabeth's stepfather heard rumours that Woolcock was enjoying sexual favours from her, he threatened to break her legs. Undeterred by the threat, she married her employer, despite warnings from her stepfather that he was a bad type of man. During this time her drug addiction continued, using morphine obtained legally from local chemists.

Woolcock, however, was strict, violent and unpredictable. He found fault with her housekeeping, and accused her of having an affair with a boarder called Tom Pascoe. Then, when his dog died suddenly, he suspected that Pascoe might have poisoned the animal. The canine's rotting body was later exhumed and tested, with high levels of mercury found in its internal organs.

Pascoe was certainly Elizabeth's co-conspirator in obtaining opium, along with a powder that was most likely precipitate of mercury. He sometimes acted as her representative, using handwritten notes in false names. Her stepson, Thomas John, was also enlisted for this purpose.

As Elizabeth later wrote: 'I was not married long, before I found out what sort of man I had got, and that my poor stepfather had advised me for my good. But was too late then so I had to make the best of it. I tried to do my duty to him and the children but the more I tried the worse he was. He was fond of drink but he did not like to part with his money for anything else and God only knows how he ill-treated me. I put up with it for three years, during that time my parents went to Melbourne and then he was worse than ever.'

Periodic attempts to leave home and run for Adelaide did not help, for Woolcock tracked her down and dragged her back. Addicted to opium, and trapped in an abusive marriage, Elizabeth tried to hang herself. The plan would have succeeded but for the weakness of the beam she tied her rope to – it broke when she kicked away her chair.

When Woolcock fell ill, Elizabeth consulted a series of doctors, giving at least the appearance of trying to save her husband. Nothing seemed to work. Thomas slid towards death, and on the 4th of September 1873 the undertaker called to collect his body.

The local rumour mill went into overdrive. After all, Elizabeth's desperate need for opiates was well known, and rumours of an affair with Tom Pascoe had kept tongues wagging for months. An inquest was convened and the finger was pointed at Elizabeth. She was charged with murdering her husband by mixing toxic mercury powder into his food, and sent to trial.

The jury had no trouble finding her guilty, and she was

sentenced to be hung by the neck until she was dead. It is ironic that Elizabeth's rapist was granted clemency, and spared the rope, but she herself was not, despite a recommendation for leniency from the jury.

Most death sentences were carried out after twenty-one days, but Elizabeth had twenty-six because they did not want to hang her on Christmas Day. On December the 30th, Elizabeth was led from her cell in the company of her last confidant, Reverend Bickford. The hangman placed a noose around her neck, allowing the regulation amount of slack, then finally released the trigger that caused the trap door to fall away. After hanging for the prescribed period of one hour, she was pronounced as deceased, then buried between the inner and outer gaol walls.

Over the years, some researchers and historians have argued that Elizabeth was convicted on the flimsiest of evidence. A petition was circulated to have her conviction posthumously quashed. The suggestion received short thrift from the attorney general, but some doubt does remain.

The physical evidence that Thomas Woolcock (and his dog) died from mercury poisoning was not conclusive by modern standards. The cause of death was initially given as 'pure exhaustion from excessive and prolonged vomiting and purging.' Mercury was found, however, in dangerous levels in his organs, particularly his stomach, much more than could be attributed to the small amount in some of the medicines he was prescribed.

A letter from Elizabeth, addressed to Reverend Bickford, was handed to the Adelaide Observer after the hanging. The newspaper published it in full, with this damning confession only adding to the public's interest in the case: 'I was so ill-treated that I was quite out of my mind and in an evil hour I yielded to the temptation. He was taken ill at the mine and came home and quarrelled with me and Satan tempted me and I gave him what I ought not.' Believers in her innocence assert that she only made the confession to impress her penitence on Reverend Bickford, who had been the minister at Moonta and whom she admired.

Whatever happened, Elizabeth was a tragic figure: the

victim of careless parenthood, a savage crime and a violent marriage. Years of substance abuse may have been her way of coping with the demons of the past. She remains the only woman to be executed by the South Australian government, and a figure of mystery, sadness, and intrigue.

A letter from Elizabeth addressed to a Reverend Bickford, who had been counselling her before her death, was handed to the Adelaide Observer after the hanging. They published it in full on January 3, 1874.

THE LAST STATEMENT AND CONFESSION OF ELISABETH WOOLCOCK.

I was born in the Burra mine in the province of South Australia in the year 1847. My parents' names were John and Elisabeth Oliver. They were Cornish. They came to this colony in 1842 but they went to Victoria in 1851. I was left without the care of a mother at the age of 4 years and I never saw her again until I was 18. My father died when I was 9 years old and I had to get my living until I was 18 and then I heard that my mother was alive and residing at Moonta Mine. She wrote me a letter asking me to come to her as she had been very unhappy about me and was very sorry for what she had done. I thought I should like to see my mother and have a home like other young girls so I gave up my situation and came to Adelaide.

My mother and my stepfather received me very kindly and I had a good home for two years. My mother and stepfather were members of the Wesleyan

Church and I became a teacher in the Sunday School for two years. At the end of that time I first saw my late husband Thomas Woolcock.

I believe my stepfather was a good man but he was very passionate and determined. My late husband was a widower with two children. His wife had been dead about eight months when I went to keep house for him against Stepfather's wishes. I kept house for him for six weeks when someone told my stepfather that I was keeping company with Thomas Woolcock. He asked me if it was true and I told him it was not but he would not believe me. He called me a liar and told me he would cripple me if I went with him any more.

I, being very self-willed, told him that I had not been with the man but I would go with him now if he asked me. This took place on the Thursday morning. I saw my husband in the evening and he asked me what was the matter and I told him what had taken place the following Sunday. He asked me to go with him for a walk instead of going to chapel.

I went and my stepfather missed me from the chapel and came to look for me and met us both together so I was afraid to go home for he had said he would break both of my legs. I was afraid he would keep his word as I never knew him to tell a wilful lie. So I went to a cousin of my husband's and stopped, and my husband asked me if I would marry him and for my word's sake I did we were married the next Sunday morning by licence after the acquaintance of seven weeks. I was not married long, before I found out what sort of man I had got, and that my poor stepfather had advised me for my good. But was too late then so I had to make the best of it. I tried to do my duty to him and the children but the more I tried the worse he was. He was fond of drink but he did not like to part with his money for anything else and God only knows how he ill-treated me. I put up with it for three years, during that time my parents went to Melbourne and then he was worse than ever. I thought I would rather die than live so I tried to put an end to myself in several different ways but thank the Lord I did not succeed in doing so.

So as he did not treat me any better and I could not live like that I thought I would leave him and get my own life. So I left him but he would not leave me alone. He came and fetched me home and then I stopped with him twelve months and I left him again with the intention of going to my mother. I only took six pounds with me.

I came down to Adelaide and I stopped with my sister. I was here in Adelaide six weeks when he came and fetched me back again. But he did not behave no better to me. I tried my best to please him but I could not. There is no foundation at all for the story about the young man called Bascoe. He was nothing to me nor did I give the poor dog any poison for I knew what power the poison had as I took it myself for some months.

I was so ill-treated that I was quite out of my mind and in an evil hour I yielded to the temptation. He was taken ill at the mine and came home and quarrelled with me and Satan tempted me and I gave him what I ought not, but I thought at the time that if I gave him time to prepare to meet his God I should not do any great crime to send him out of the world.

But I see my mistake now. I thank God he had time to make his peace with his maker and I hope I shall meet him in heaven for I feel that God has pardoned all my sins. He has forgiven me and washed me white in the precious blood of Jesus. I feel this evening that I can rejoice in a loving Saviour. I feel his presence here tonight. He sustains me and gives me comfort under this heavy trial such as the world can never give.

Dear friend if I may call you so, I am much obliged to you for your kindness to a poor guilty sinner, but great will be your reward in heaven. I hope I shall meet you there, and I hope that God will keep me faithful to the end so may be able to say that live is Christ but to Die will be gain (sic). Bless the Lord he will not torn away any that come unto him for he says come onto me all ye that labour and are heavy laden and I will give you rest. I feel I have that rest.

I hope to die singing victory through the blood of the lamb. I remain sir, yours truly a sinner saved by grace.

Elizabeth Woolcock

Alma McGee

Back in the 1920s, mental illness was seen as shameful. Sufferers were locked away, and subjected to 'treatments' based on barely tested theories. The story of Alma McGee is a case in point.

Alma's mother, Frances, came from a Protestant family – landed gentry in Cork, Ireland. Frances fell in love with the Catholic stable boy, Bartholomew Murphy. Disgraced and disowned, Frances was six months pregnant when the young couple boarded the SS Whampoa, bound for Sydney.

Thirteen years later, Alma was born in James St, Newtown. Tragedy seemed to dog her life right from the start. When she was ten her older sister Florence died of a heart infection. One year later her father, the stableboy turned hansom cab driver, also died, at the age of 48.

Just 12 years old, Alma left school to work as a machinist – highly skilled work performed on lathes – and eventually married bootmaker Robert McGee. By the end of the First World War, however, Alma was troubled by nerves, exhaustion and stomach complaints. The death of her nephew Maxwell, aged just 8 months, didn't help her state of mind.

Alma's first two daughters, Ivy and Maude, were born during this time, but then, just five days before the birth of her third child, Joyce, her husband Robert McGee was taken by the influenza scourge that was raking the country. For the next twelve months Alma battled the same flu that had killed her husband, along with 'shock' and 'nervous turns' while her mother, Frances, helped care for the girls.

Despite a succession of tragedies, including her brother dying from pueripheral neuritis, in Rockwood Asylum, Alma was again, in 1923, engaged to be married. Yet, on the cusp of her wedding it was revealed that her husband-to-be was already married. The wedding could not proceed.

This must have seemed like a last straw. Alma, now the recipient of an invalid pension, was bedridden with ulcers, eating disorders, and anxiety.

At the age of 35 Alma was admitted to Royal Prince Alfred Hospital, then Broughton Hall Psychiatric Clinic, and Gladesville Mental Hospital. She was an inmate of these institutions, on and off, for years. The diagnosis given was 'Hysteria', 'Melancholia Delusiona', and later as 'Manic Depressive Psychosis'.

Well meaning but brutal treatments were the order of the day. Under the teachings of an American psychiatrist, Dr Cotton, teeth were seen as a source of bacteria and thus a cause of insanity. All of Alma's teeth were removed and she was fed via a nasal tube while the stumps healed.

Alma was not allowed to see her children, adding to the 'hysteria' that she was being treated for.

Meanwhile the three girls lived with their grandparents until their death, at which stage Ivy, the eldest, acted as head of the family, supporting her two younger sisters both financially and emotionally. They lived in a tiny but spotless house in Canterbury, Sydney.

After six years in mental institutions, Alma was allowed to return home to live with her daughters. Ivy was by then a capable young woman of 20 years. But still Alma was periodically forced to return to the asylums where she had spent so much of her adult life, despite Ivy's pleas to keep her at home.

The final chapter in Alma's life was both happy and tragic. At the age of 49 she married Jim Parks, at St George's

Church, Earlwood. They moved into a flat at the back of a family home in Canterbury.

Unfortunately, some 15 months later, Alma suffered a serious bout of flu. A doctor was called but he could not come. She died the next day in an ambulance on her way to the hospital. She was 50 years old.

Postscript: Alma was my great-grandmother. My mother, Faye, oldest child of Alma's youngest daughter Joyce, remembered her as kind and loving. She also had fond memories of 'Poppa Jim', Alma's husband for those few short months.

Most of the research for this story was undertaken by Barbara Moules, Joyce's second daughter.

POETS AND WORDSMITHS

Steele Rudd

It's twenty years ago now since we settled on the Creek. Twenty years! I remember well the day we came from Stanthorpe, on Jerome's dray – eight of us, and all the things – beds, tubs, a bucket, the two cedar chairs with the pine bottoms and backs that Dad put in them, some pint-pots and old Crib. It was a scorching hot day, too – talk about thirst! At every creek we came to we drank till it stopped running.

So begins the first-ever published story by Steele Rudd, featuring the wonderful Australian characters Dad and Dave. But Steele Rudd's real name was Arthur Hoey Davis, and his life was just as interesting as those of his famous characters.

Born in 1868, Arthur Davis was six years old when he and his brothers and sisters, walking beside a cart piled high with furniture and farm equipment, arrived at 'Shingle Hut' on the Darling Downs, there to make their fortune. 'Dad' had arrived a few weeks earlier and knocked up a rough slab hut. Before long, through drought, flood and very occasional plenty the family had swelled to thirteen children.

The young Arthur, was, according to a much later recollection by his son Eric:

> *Six feet tall – active and athletic – his carriage was erect – also his seat on horseback. He had a ruddy complexion with twinkling brown eyes – keenly alert and observant, with wrinkles at his temples which lent a humorous outlook. Kindness was one of his virtues, and he was generous to the extreme.*

At the local school, Emu Creek, Arthur was quiet and hard working. There was one little girl who liked to sit with him in the playground, and talk about horses, dogs and books. Her name was Christina Brodie, always called 'Tean' for short.

By the age of twelve Arthur had finished school and was earning a living 'picking up' at the woolshed on nearby Pilton Station, and honing his skills as a jockey at the local picnic races. After a stint as a drover 'out west' his mother arranged for him to apply for the civil service. His application was successful and he soon found himself in the foreign world of turn-of-the-century Brisbane.

Arthur's first city job was with the office of the Curator

of Intestate Estates, and a later book called 'The Miserable Clerk' gives a clue to what he thought of this situation. A flatmate, however, got him into reading Charles Dickens, and his interest in rowing led to him writing a series of articles under the pen name 'Steele Rudder,' later changed to 'Steele Rudd.'

After a few years in the city he missed the bush life so much that he began to read everything he could about the outback. Eventually, he had a go at writing his own stories. His first sketch of life growing up in his boisterous family, 'Starting the Selection,' was published in the Bulletin Magazine in 1895, championed by J.F. Archibald, the force behind so much great Australian literature.

That same year, Arthur headed back home and asked his childhood sweetheart, Christina, to marry him. She was full of fun and good sense, and had a keen editing pen. It was 'Tean' who first read and helped hone Arthur's early stories.
'On Our Selection' was published in full by the Bulletin Magazine in 1899, followed by 'Our New Selection' in 1903. Both won popular and critical acclaim. Two of the main characters, Dad and Dave, became part of Australian folklore.
Partly through jealousy at his success, Arthur was retrenched from his public service job, and responded by moving to Sydney and starting his own magazine. Nothing could keep him down. As his son Eric later said of him: 'He was always a man's man, tough, testy, a good friend.'
All was not well with Tean. The lack of a steady family income tested her disposition. The magazine slowly dropped in sales, then was forced to close, making her state of mind worse. Believing that a big change might help, Arthur took the family back home to the Darling Downs, settling on a property called 'The Firs,' where he bred polo ponies and entered local politics, becoming head of the Cambooya Shire Council.
During World War One their son Gower was badly injured at the Somme, and Tean's 'frailty' became full blown men-

tal illness. The family were forced to sell up and move to Brisbane where she could receive special care. She was hospitalised permanently in 1919, but lived on for more than twenty years.

'Steele Rudd' never stopped writing until his death in 1935, but made little money in his later years. A grateful nation endowed him with a 'literary pension' to the tune of twenty-five shillings per week, for which he was apparently grateful.

Arthur published many other books and stories over his lifetime, including that ill-fated magazine, but nothing ever approached the freshness and honesty of his first two works, On our Selection, and Our new Selection. They are true classics, and an insight into how life was, 'back then.'

Where the Dead Men Lie

There have always been two opposing views on the nature of the Australian bush: epitomised in the romantic world of Banjo Patterson, and the harder, more brutal outback of Henry Lawson.

The poet who presented the bush in the harshest light of all was stockman and poet Barcroft Boake. That doesn't, of course, mean that he loved it any less. Born in Balmain, in 1866, Barcroft was the son of a very early professional photographer. Having lost three of his siblings in their infancy, he was prone to bouts of melancholy, even as a child, but he loved sport and outdoor activities. He dreamed of living and working in the outback.

At the age of seventeen Barcroft applied for training as a surveyor. He spent years in the back blocks of New South Wales, connecting with the Western landscape. Before long he had quit the Survey Department and was off droving in Queensland. At the same time he devoured the poetry of Adam Lindsay Gordon, and developed the urge to express the tough love he felt for the bush. He started writing, and by 1890 his poems were appearing regularly in the Bulletin magazine.

His career as a poet was short-lived. When he was just twenty-four years of age he was called back to Sydney where his family was facing bankruptcy. Barcroft helped with what he could, but fruitlessly searched for work, battling depression and anxiety. His body was found under a tree on the shores of Sydney Harbour in May 1892, hanging from his own stockwhip.

Where the Dead Men Lie
By Barcroft Boake

Out on the wastes of the Never Never -
That's where the dead men lie!
There where the heat-waves dance forever -
That's where the dead men lie!
That's where the Earth's loved sons are keeping
Endless tryst: not the west wind sweeping
Feverish pinions can wake their sleeping -
Out where the dead men lie!

Where brown Summer and Death have mated -
That's where the dead men lie!
Loving with fiery lust unsated -
That's where the dead men lie!
Out where the grinning skulls bleach whitely
Under the saltbush sparkling brightly;
Out where the wild dogs chorus nightly -
That's where the dead men lie!

Deep in the yellow, flowing river -
That's where the dead men lie!
Under the banks where the shadows quiver -
That's where the dead men he!

*Where the platypus twists and doubles,
Leaving a train of tiny bubbles.
Rid at last of their earthly troubles -
That's where the dead men lie!*

*East and backward pale faces turning -
That's how the dead men lie!
Gaunt arms stretched with a voiceless yearning -
That's how the dead men lie!
Oft in the fragrant hush of nooning
Hearing again their mother's crooning,
Wrapt for aye in a dreamful swooning -
That's how the dead men lie!*

*Only the hand of Night can free them -
That's when the dead men fly!
Only the frightened cattle see them -
See the dead men go by!
Cloven hoofs beating out one measure,
Bidding the stockmen know no leisure -
That's when the dead men take their pleasure!
That's when the dead men fly!*

*Ask, too, the never-sleeping drover:
He sees the dead pass by;
Hearing them call to their friends - the plover,
Hearing the dead men cry;
Seeing their faces stealing, stealing,
Hearing their laughter, pealing, pealing,
Watching their grey forms wheeling, wheeling
Round where the cattle lie!*

*Strangled by thirst and fierce privation -
That's how the dead men die!
Out on Moneygrub's farthest station -
That's how the dead men die!
Hard-faced greybeards, youngsters callow;
Some mounds cared for, some left fallow;*

Some deep down, yet others shallow.
Some having but the sky.

Moneygrub, as he sips his claret,
Looks with complacent eye
Down at his watch-chain, eighteen carat -
There, in his club, hard by:
Recks not that every link is stamped with
Names of the men whose limbs are cramped with
Too long lying in grave-mould, cramped with
Death where the dead men lie.

Edward Dickens

Not many people know that the youngest son of one of the great English novelists, Charles Dickens, lies at rest in the cemetery of an Australian outback town.

Edward Dickens was encouraged by his father to migrate to Australia, where he took to farm and station life as if he was born to it. He became manager of Momba Station near Wilcannia and married a local girl. In and out of financial trouble for much of his life, he had an interest in several "runs", and became an alderman on the Bourke Shire Council, a booming region in the day.

Stints as a land and rabbit inspector led to a long period of ill-health and unemployment. He died in Moree in 1902, aged just fifty. His gravestone still stands in the cemetery there.

EXPLORERS AND CATTLE KINGS

Jack and Kate

John Warrington Rogers was the eldest son of a politician and QC from Tasmania and Victoria. Young 'Jack' as he was called, was sent 'home' to England to attend an expensive private school, but he wanted no truck with balls and banquets. As soon as he returned to Australia, he saddled a horse and rode off for the outback, setting in train a fifty-year story of bush life, cattle station management, a real-life love affair, and a series of tragedies.

In Queensland Jack soon proved himself as a top cattleman. Not surprisingly, as he was a strongly built man – six feet tall, and was taught to ride not long after he could walk. He loved horses, wide open spaces and adventure in equal measure, cutting his teeth in tough Western Queensland stock camps.

Meanwhile, his younger brothers followed carefully planned careers in law and the military. Jack's brother Cyril was a Lance Corporal in the Imperial Light Infantry, fighting in the Boer War. He was killed in action at the Battle of Spion Kop at just twenty-one years of age.

War, however, seemed a long way off when Jack was stringing cattle along the Georgina River. There he met Catherine Matilda McCaw, the eldest daughter of James

McCaw, of Urandangi, Queensland. Nineteen years younger than Jack, Catherine was known universally as Kate, blue eyed and full of life.

Jack invited her to a dance in Boulia. Kate replied that she'd rather just get on with it, and why didn't he just ask her to marry him straight off?

Kate proudly took her father's arm as he led her down the aisle in Camooweal. It was 1901, the year Australia became a nation. The few members of the Rogers family who made the trek lent a fashionable air to the proceedings, with their dark suits and the latest dresses.

Arafura Swamp (NT Library)

When Jack headed to the Territory, and up into Arnhem Land, to manage Joe Bradshaw's newly formed Arafura Station, he couldn't have had a better woman beside him. Kate Rodgers had grown up in the bush. She was a born horsewoman, great with a rifle, and an expert at managing stockmen of all personalities and backgrounds.

The Northern Territory Times and Gazette reported, on their arrival, that Kate was 'generally regarded as a better cattle manager than Jack.' And Jack made no secret of his plan to appoint her as head stockman.

Glenville Pike, in his book, Frontier Territory, described Kate as:

> An expert in the stock camp or on horseback, she was also a crack shot with rifle or revolver. Old timers have told of Kate Rogers's everyday life — dashing through the timber and long grass

on a galloping horse, skirts flying and with stock whip thundering, horse and rider moving as one, as she wheeled a mob of wild long horned cattle. Arafura Station was no picnic, operating on a scarcely believable ten thousand square miles of what is now East Arnhem Land. Wetland cattle management was difficult in the Dry Season, impossible in the Wet. The station homestead was located on the Glyde River, not far from the present day settlement of Ramingining. Mosquitoes, cattle-spearing locals, humidity, heat, crocodiles, and rain all counted against the station's success.

The homestead came under determined attack several times. On one occasion two of the Chinese gardeners were speared, and Kate was forced to barricade herself inside, armed with her '73 Winchester. She was supported by the station cook, firing an ancient blunderbuss, holding out until Jack and the men came home.

Their son John (also nicknamed Jack) was born in 1902, but Kate didn't let him slow her down – she'd carry him in a sling around her neck while she got on with station duties.

Like Florida Station, operating on pretty much the same area some twenty years earlier, Arafura Station was ultimately abandoned, and the remaining cattle transferred to another Bradshaw property. The country was just too harsh and too remote, and the Traditional Owners, justifiably, fought hard to keep the whites and their cattle out.

The first chapter of their lives was closed. But the impact of this remarkable couple on the Northern Territory pastoral industry was only just beginning. Undeterred, Jack reformed Paddy's Lagoon Station, bordered by the Roper and Wilton Rivers. This was drier, more forgiving country, with some excellent pasture. While they were there Kate gave birth to a daughter, but unfortunately she passed away on the same day. The small grave did not remain alone for long: Jack's brother Harry, who came to stay with them after the collapse of his business interests, died of typhoid fever there in 1909.

Jack was a talented cattleman and sharp businessman, always with an eye for opportunities. He reformed Paddy's Lagoon into Urapunga Station, then set up Maryfield in partnership with a man named Farrar.

Kate continued to run the station cattle yards, horse paddocks and drove 'fats' to market. On at least one occasion, while Jack was busy running the station, Kate left her infant with a nanny, and, with a plant of horses and half a dozen men, drove a mob of bullocks to Camooweal.

For many years she was assisted by a capable Aboriginal woman known as Princess Polly. Kate's son John could ride before he learned to read or write.

Kate was not only as capable as any man in the yards, but she was also a sympathetic woman who formed a genuine love for the Aboriginal people of the north.

While living with Jack at Hodgson Downs Station, which he was managing, she worked with Archbishop Gilbert White on the formation of the Roper River Mission. This was not merely a paternalistic gesture. The Indigenous people of the region were shattered and cowed from years of violent confrontation: leprosy was common, with a weekly truck shipping sufferers up to a colony at Channel Island. Addiction to opium, imported and sold by the Chinese, was also a problem, more usually back near the railway line and mining areas. The mission was an attempt to protect and consolidate the people of the Roper Valley before it was too late.

Possibly under the influence of Jack's father, young John was eventually sent off to private school in Melbourne. And with only five mail deliveries on the station each year, contact with their son was rare. In 1914, at the height of the wet season, Jack was away when Kate received a telegram from 'down south' stating that their son was seriously ill, and asking for his parents' permission for the doctors to operate.

Knowing full well that every creek and river between home and Katherine, including the mighty Roper, was in flood, Kate was determined to reach the telegraph station there. With a couple of loyal horsemen, and fully-laden packhorses for the journey, Kate set out on a journey to save her son.

Kate and Workers

That trip to Katherine must have been a nightmare: fighting humid heat and mosquitoes, fording swollen rivers and driving the packhorses through driving rain and bogs. Two weeks of travel later, they swam their horses across the flooded Katherine River at the Springvale Crossing (now known as the Low Level). By then, almost a month had passed since the original message was sent.

Waiting for Kate at the post office, however, was a new telegram telling her that the doctors had operated regardless and that young John had fully recovered. It was a wasted trip, but Kate's smile must have been a mile wide as she took the opportunity to buy stores and meet old friends.

Before long, John's schooling was over, and there was no question of a fancy career for him. It was the station life he wanted, and the small family were soon together again.

As the new decade, the 1920s arrived, Jack sold Maryfield Station and, flush with cash, announced a family holiday. Jack, Kate and John steamed south on SS Bambra. What was meant to be a pleasant interlude, however, turned into a tragedy.

While in Victoria, Kate grew sick with pneumonia. Jack was at her side to the end, praying for her not to die, wondering how the hell he could possibly live without her.

The incredible Kate Rogers, who had faced down charging bulls, uncountable lonely nights on the track, and wild Top End cyclones, fell to a microscopic bug in her lungs. She died in Brighton, Victoria at the age of 45, and is buried in the cemetery there.

Kate's obituary in Darwin's Northern Standard newspaper read:

> *(Kate Rogers) was a woman of exceptional ability, and she will be remembered in the outback parts of the Territory for her skill and courage in everything pertaining to the management of the station, and for her generosity and great kindness of heart.*

Heartbroken, Jack returned to the north with his son, operating Roper Valley Station and Urapunga before selling the latter station. For a while his heart went out of it, but he had to think of his son's future.

In 1925 Jack and John were among the first NT pastoralists to ship live bullocks to Indonesia and the Philippines. Jack was also, by nature of his importance to the Roper area, appointed as a Justice of the Peace by the Government Resident.

As he neared seventy years of age Jack was still a fearless horseman and consummate bushman. In 1927, he was droving one hundred head of fat bullocks, single handed, to the butcher supplying crews laying the railway line from Katherine to Daly Waters. Jack's horse tripped and fell, trapping him underneath and breaking bones in his leg, thigh and hip. The cattle wandered off, leaving him alone, an old man, with crippling injuries. Yet, Jack's unerring sense of direction told him the nearest place of safety: the Presbyterian Inland Mission at Maranboy.

For five days he crawled towards his destination, fighting off the dingoes and kite hawks that waited for him to fall. Somehow, through determination and strength of mind, he got there, and a Dr Kirklands was dispatched by train to treat him. Unfortunately the injuries left him partially crippled, but he was still vital and thirsting for life.

Official obituaries don't mention this fact. But Jack found love again, from a local Roper woman. In around 1930, well advanced in years, Jack became a father for the third time. His girl child was healthy and vital, and must have been a comfort in his sunset years.

In 1931 Jack purchased Urapunga Station for the second time, a brave move for a seventy-four year old. His holdings were then around three thousand square miles on both sides of the Roper River. But the Great Depression was sucking the life out of every enterprise, in every nation. Cattle prices dropped to uneconomic levels.

Close to bankruptcy, in 1934, Jack sold Roper Valley Station to the Royallison Pastoral Company for a fraction of its value. He was finished, riding away with just a horse and the clothes on his back. How that must have hurt after being the boss man for so long! He farewelled young John, who had his pick of job offers on other stations, and went to the Mataranka Hotel to drown his sorrows.

In 1935, at the age of 78, still at Mataranka, Jack borrowed a rifle, and shot himself in the head. The wound was not immediately fatal, and that tough old man took sixteen hours to die. Dr Clyde Fenton, the Territory's first flying doctor, arrived in time to issue the death certificate.

Jack's obituary in the Northern Standard Newspaper stated:

> *The passing of John Warrington Rogers at Mataranka on Tuesday morning last at the age of 74 (sic) removes from the ranks of the northern pastoralists one of nature's gentlemen with a history of fine achievements in the development of the Northern Territory.*

Sadly, this tragedy of Jack and Kate had one more act to play.

Their son John was mustering on Victoria River Downs Station in 1943 when his horse fell and rolled on him, leaving him with severe head injuries. He died three days later.

Jack's daughter, who I won't name for cultural reasons, became an elder of her people, living at a Roper community. She died in 2008 and is survived by her many children, grandchildren and great grandchildren.

Nat Buchanan

When Irishman, Lieutenant Charles Henry Buchanan and his wife, Annie, emigrated to Australia and took up a New England station called Rimbanda, they had no idea that their son Nathaniel would one day become known as the greatest drover the world has ever seen. Nat grew from a cheerful and adventurous lad into a competent man, with an even temper, incredible organisational skills and an unerring sense of direction. Nat 'Bluey' Buchanan was a bushman par excellence with a passion for new horizons. He single-handedly opened up more country than some of our most famous explorers.

In 1861, for example, Nat Buchanan and his business partner Edward Cornish were out exploring in Western Queensland. Having taken up land to create Bowen Downs Station, they decided to poke around much further to the west. Penetrating all the way to the Diamantina River they discovered the tracks of a camel train. The tracks were, it turned out, made by one of the most expensive expeditions in the history of white exploration: Burke and Wills on their way from the Cooper Creek Depot to the Gulf of Carpentaria. That Buchanan and Cornish came upon those famous men and their entourage, while 'poking around' out west, with just one tracker and some packhorses, is a good illustration of the difference between independent bushmen and government sponsored explorers.

A few years earlier, Nat's working life started out with the taking up of a station north of Guyra called Bald Blair, in partnership with his brothers Andrew and Frank. The trio also embarked on an unsuccessful trip to the Californian goldfields. When they returned, Bald Blair was laden with debt and had to be sold.

Nat polished up his droving skills, taking herds of sheep or cattle to the goldfields and interstate, following this profession for at least a decade before heading for Queensland and the vast frontier. His first real foray into Western Queensland was from Rockhampton with William Landsborough in 1860. Within a year they had formed Bowen Downs station on the Thomson River, and Nat was installed as manager.

Nat met the attractive brunette Catherine Gordon when by chance he rode into her family's campsite, on the Burnett River near Rockhampton. According to Bobbie Buchanan, Nat's grand-daughter, Kate was 'a natural horsewoman, and an accomplished rider.' She was also a stunning young woman, and Nat was captivated.

The young couple were married soon after, and Nat took his bride out to Bowen Downs in a buggy.

Married or not, Buchanan had no intention of living a settled life. After checking out much of Western Queensland he started exploring the Gulf country around Burketown, looking for suitable pastoral land for his business partners.

The strain of constant travel did tell on him, and Kate was by then pleading for some normality. In 1870 Nat and his brother Andrew took up a selection of land on Deep Creek, near Valla, NSW. This was still wild country then, frequented by cedar-getters and fugitives. The brothers and their families built bark and slab houses on the river bank, where they raised goats and chickens, planted a few acres of corn and cleared land for cattle. The plentiful fish in the creek varied the diet nicely.

Kate Buchanan

Essential supplies were purchased via a fifty-mile ride to Kempsey, and mail was delivered into a letterbox nailed to a tree on Valla Beach, accessible by a long row downstream. Kate must have hoped that her man had grown roots, but Nat's adventurous years were barely getting started.

Pining for open country, and sick of the humidity, Nat moved Kate and their sons Gordon and Wattie north again. He managed Craven Station for a while, then took on his first big droving contracts. He was the first European to cross the Barkly Tablelands in 1877, sparking an explosion of land speculation. Most lease contracts, moreover, stipulated that the run had be stocked within two years. The owners were crying out for cattle and men to drove them.

Now in his fifties, Nat led the largest cattle drive in history – 20 000 head from St George in Queensland to Glencoe in the Northern Territory. He made the record books again a few years later, delivering the first cattle to the East Kimberley. One of his most harrowing achievements was the blazing of the bleak Murranji Track, from near Daly Waters to Victoria River Downs.

Nat's descendant and biographer, Bobbie Buchanan, described him as a 'confident, strong-willed and uniquely self-sufficient man of great integrity.' His organisational skills were legendary, and his ability to keep tough men on track and working together no less impressive.

Nat Buchanan's rules on cattle drives were inviolate:

1) Travel at speed. This was a technique he referred to as, 'giving the cattle the gooseberry,' or just 'the old gooseberry.'

2) No alcohol in camp. In 1883 when he took over a drive to the Kimberley for W.H. Osmand and JA Panton, his first act was to tip out the demijohns of rum he found hidden in the drays. He was a teetotaller himself, and knew well the effect of grog in cattle camps.

3) Never let wild Aborigines into a camp, male or female.

4) No man should be left in camp alone.

On a drive through the Gulf in 1878, Nat was forced to head back to Normanton for provisions. He was away for some weeks, and the man he left in charge, Charles Bridson, relaxed these last two rules. Some very insistent Aborigines who knew a few words of pidgin talked their way into the camp. This error was compounded when Bridson rode off and left another man, Travers, alone in the camp.

Travers was making damper, dusted to the elbows in flour, when a steel hatchet that had been lying around the camp cleaved deep into the back of his skull. The event set off days of drama and revenge killings. Buchanan, on his return, was understandably incensed.

Nat's next plan was to bring his family together on one of the largest cattle runs in history – Wave Hill Station – one of several leases Nat took up in partnership with his brother. Unfortunately the skills that made him a great drover and adventurer did not extend to management. Distance to markets and attacks on stock by the local Gurindji people were the two most important issues.

Nat, by the way, was known for a generally conciliatory approach to Aboriginal people, and was spoken of fondly by Indigenous workers in oral histories from the region. Cattle, fences and men were not welcomed by traditional owners – the Europeans were invaders after all – and conflict was a fact of the frontier. Buchanan, however, was never party to the 'shoot on sight' mentality of some frontiersmen.

In the 1920s Territory bushman, and chronicler Tom Cole came across an old Jingali man on Wave Hill Station, who the whites called Charcoal. Charcoal had worked on Wave Hill and in droving camps with Nat Buchanan as a boy and young man.

During an attack by wild blacks on the station, Charcoal used his rifle to shoot one attacker out of a tree. Bluey Buchanan, or Old Paraway, as his men called him, was furious, Charcoal had never seen him so angry. 'You shot one of the poor bastards dead?' Bluey roared. 'Jesus Christ! You shouldn't have done that!'

Even at the age of seventy Nat was out exploring again, searching for a stock route from the Barkly Tableland to Western Australia. His health was poor by then, and in 1899 he retired to a small property near Walcha, New South Wales, with his beloved and long-suffering Kate. Originally buried at Dungowan, his remains were later moved to Walcha. His gravestone takes pride of place in the cemetery, along with a plaque commemorating his life.

The most fitting epitaph for this great man is perhaps the words some of his contemporaries wrote about him. Charlie Gaunt stated: 'Buchanan had the gift of bushmanship and location. He was a fine, genial companion to have;

you only had to look at Nat Buchanan to see in his physique, actions and general appearance a thorough typical bushman with the face showing dogged determination and strong will power; one who would stand by you until the bells of eternity rang.'

Stockman Billy Linklater, in his memoir, Gather No Moss, wrote of Nat Buchanan: 'His willpower was indomitable, yet he was mild-mannered and of a most kindly disposition.'

Finally, in the words of singer/songwriter Ted Egan (who was present at the ceremony marking the reburying of Nat's remains next to his wife in Walcha):

> *Nat Buchanan, old Bluey, old Paraway*
> *What would you think if you came back today?*
> *It's not as romantic as in your time, Old Nat,*
> *Not many drovers and we're sad about that.*
> *Fences and bitumen and road trains galore.*
> *Oh they move cattle quicker, but one thing is sure*
> *Road trains go faster, but of drovers we sing*
> *And everyone knows Nat Buchanan was King.*

Captain Joe Bradshaw

Joe Bradshaw was one of the most adventurous of the early Northern Australian pastoralists.

He was born in Melbourne in 1855 with cattle and farming in his blood. His father owned several properties in Victoria, including Bolwarra and Bacchus Marsh Stations.

An explorer by nature, by his early twenties, 'Captain' Joe Bradshaw was plying the waters of Northern Australia in a schooner named *Twins*. He was particularly interested in the Kimberley district, finding excellent pastoral lands along the Prince Regent River, where he took up a score of 50 000 acre blocks. Naming the station Marigui, he set out to build the property into a pastoral showpiece.

Trips 'back south' to raise money for his enterprises were interspersed with problems, such as the WA government hiking fees to such a level as to make new cattle enterprises uneconomic, and his first choice of stock – sheep – proving to be unsuited to the conditions. He also once returned to the then bustling town of Wyndham to find that it had been ravaged by a cyclone.

Joe's cousin, Aeneus Gunn, was one of a number of friends and family who arrived to manage stations and businesses on Joe's behalf. The future wife of Aeneus, Jeannie Gunn, much later wrote the Australian classic, We of the Never Never.

Joe's love affair with the Victoria River district began with a trip up that mighty river in a steamer called *Red Gauntlet*. The trip was ostensibly to drop a Government exploration party upriver, but Joe was impressed with the beauty of the mountains with their sheer cliffs, and the Mitchell grass plains. In partnership with his older brother Fred, Joe took up 20 000 square miles encompassing almost all the land between the Victoria and Fitzmaurice Rivers, and all the way west to the sea.

Bradshaw Station (NLA)

On a trip 'down south' Joe fell in love with a young woman called Mary Guy, and married her on a trip to Melbourne in 1891. During 1893 Mary delivered two children, William Guy and Jas, both dying in infancy.

More disaster followed when Joe's brother and business partner Fred was travelling from the Victoria River to Port Darwin in his oil-powered launch, the *Bolwarra*, with two friends and a Russian engineer. They called in at Port Keats near the mouth of the Daly where their Aboriginal 'boys' deserted. A new crew were persuaded to join them, but that night, while the white men slept, anchored off Point Cook, they were bashed to death with clubs.

An expedition led by a policeman called Kelly found the launch drifting, damaged and bloody, and most of the bodies on the shore nearby. They were buried on a sandy beach, but for Joe Bradshaw this wasn't a fitting resting place for the older brother he loved.

Joe had a number of coffins made, and travelled by lugger to the site. Bodies of the other members of the party were presumably repatriated to Darwin, but Joe had special plans for Fred. He carried his brother's body back to the big river. The cliff top Joe chose was too solid to dig a hole, so Fred was laid to rest under a cairn on a high cliff, now known as Bradshaw's Tomb, overlooking one of Australia's most beautiful river valleys.

Even then, despite a diagnosis of diabetes, and Mary returning 'South' to supervise their son's education, Joe did not slow down. He was pivotal in the formation of a company called the Eastern and African Cold Storage Supply Company.

This company managed, through lobbying and powerful friends, to obtain leases and other arrangements to use the eastern half of Arnhem Land as their private domain. Before long, the area was running up to 17 000 head of cattle in the face of determined resistance from local Traditional Owners. Like previous attempts to use this area for pastoral purposes, Arafura Station was ultimately a failure. (See the Jack and Kate story for more on this)

In 1916 Joe sustained a wound in his foot, which soon turned septic. Lying incapacitated in Darwin Hospital, Joe's last wish was that he be buried next to his brother, under a cairn of stone on the hill called Bradshaw's Tomb on the Victoria River.

According to an obituary: 'There are many worse men in the world than the late 'Captain' Joe Bradshaw. Whilst he had his faults and weaknesses, he was a kindly and courteous gentleman at heart, absolutely 'straight' in all his dealings with his fellow men.'

Joe Bradshaw was a one-of-a-kind. Coming from a background of wealth, he had the funds to treat Northern Australia as a playground, notwithstanding the isolation and hardship he must have endured at times. He was a long-time member of the Royal Geographical Society of London and is credited with being the first white man to view the Gwion Gwion style of indigenous art, which was named after him for many years. Yet, for all that, brutal deeds were done in his name, and at heart Joe Bradshaw was ultimately concerned with making money and empire building.

Joe's wish to be buried beside his brother on that Victoria River cliff top remains unfulfilled. His grave can be found at the Darwin Pioneer cemetery at Palmerston, south of Darwin. Mary outlived her husband by 26 years, passing away in 1942 at Kew, Victoria. Bradshaw Station is now a Royal Australian Air Force Testing Range.

Bradshaw's Tomb (NLA)

Carrie Creaghe

Women in the Victorian era were often sheltered and protected, dominated by strict male figures and lacking experience in the real world. Yet, not all women were like that. There were female outlaws, ship's captains, drovers, and even the odd well-bred adventurer like Carrie Creagh, probably the first European female to cross the Gulf of Carpentaria.

Emily Caroline Creaghe, usually known as Carrie, was born in 1860 on a boat in the Bay of Bengal, India. Her father was a Major in the Royal Artillery, and her relatives included a Marquis and State Governors. Moving to Australia with her family at a young age, at 21 she married station manager Harry Creaghe, who was jealous of his friend Ernest Favenc's explorations across Northern Australia.

'Feel like going on one of Ernest's trips?' Harry asked her.

'Why not?' she said, and preparations began.

Over six months in the saddle, in the wild upper Macarthur River area and beyond, Carrie learned to love the bush. A swag shared with her husband each night was her home. The two fell deeper in love over time, though Carrie clashed repeatedly with Favenc, who she called 'Grumpy.' It was a harsh trip, with conditions that killed at least one of the white males on the trip. It also earned Carrie the tag of 'Australia's first female explorer.'

Returning to outback Queensland, Carrie gave birth to two children, Gerald and Harry Junior. Sadly, however, her husband died in a tragic accident. Not a woman to sit around grieving, Carrie found and married a new man: Joseph Barnett.

In 1899 she was on her way to New Zealand with five of her children. The ship, called the *Perthshire*, broke a propeller shaft and drifted the seas for seven weeks. With the ship's supplies of food and water soon exhausted, Carrie kept her brood alive until they were finally rescued.

Carrie bred half a dozen strong and adventurous children. Two sons served in France in World War. Only one returned.

Carrie died, matriarch of a loving family, in 1944.

Charles Fisher

Most Australians know the names of our biggest cattle kings, Sidney Kidman and John Cox. Charles Brown Fisher was in the same league, building an empire of land, men, cattle and sheep when things were much tougher.

Charles was born in 1818, in London. Feeling restricted by city life, as a young man he moved to Northamptonshire to work on his uncle's farm, loving country life. When his parents and eight siblings decided to emigrate to Australia, the young Charles couldn't get on the ship quick enough.

Settling with the family in Adelaide, Charles and his three brothers joined their father as stock agents and carriers, but that was never going to be enough for Charles. He was soon running sheep and cattle along the Little Para River, then stocked a large tract from what is now Parafield Airport to the meatworks at Gepps Cross.

After taking control of a swathe of properties, in 1856 the Fisher Brothers partnership sheared 115 000 sheep, and sent an unknown number of cattle to the slaughterhouse.

Charles's mother, Elizabeth, died in 1857, and just two years later his brothers George and Hurtle were transporting three racehorses on a coastal steamer, *Admella*, when it struck rocks off Port Macdonnell. Hurtle and George paddled together in the water, clinging to debris, waiting for a rescue ship that came too late. George slipped beneath the cold waters while his brother watched helplessly on.

By then Charles was living mainly in St Kilda, Melbourne. He was a regular at Flemington Racecourse, his own horses winning regularly on the track. Around this time he wooed and married Agnes Louisa Peckham. They had just one child, also named Charles.

Meanwhile, Fisher was forging one of Australia's biggest land empires.

He soon owned huge tracts of land across South Australia and Victoria, including some of the country's most valuable racehorse studs. He had leases on sixteen Queensland Stations, and with new partner JC Lyon pressed on into the Northern Territory. Glencoe Station was the Territory's first big cattle run, and Charles engaged the best in the business, Nat Buchanan, to drove the first mob, 1200 cattle from Aramac in Queensland. Later Nat would, on Charles's orders, undertake the biggest cattle drive in world history, 20 000 head from St George in Southern Queensland to Glencoe. (NB: Charlie Gaunt was also on that drive)

Fisher's ambition had no limits, and together with Lyon he obtained a lease on a huge area of land that became Victoria River Downs, at various times the biggest cattle station in the world. This was the jewel in the crown of Fisher's ambitions, then covering more than 40 000 square kilometres.

At the peak of his expansion Charles Fisher controlled more country than most European kings.

In the 1890s the empire fell apart. With beef sales in decline and general recession, the complicated financial structure Charles had built began to unravel. By 1895 he was declared bankrupt, though he was able to retain a residence and enough income to live on.

Charles's beloved Agnes died aged 60, in November 1906. Charles lived on for another 18 months, passing away in his home on Albert Terrace, Glenelg. His grave still stands at the West Terrace Cemetery, Adelaide.

SHIPS AND SEAFARERS

Sixty Ships and One Thousand Men.

The extent of the Macassar penetration into Northern Australia was greater than is generally acknowledged: much more than a few scattered trepang-seeking proas. In fact, as this excerpt from Voyage to Terra Australia by Matthew Flinders, shows, Macassar incursions featured large numbers of boats and men; heavily armed and organised on military lines. The following meeting took place on the coast of Eastern Arnhem Land, not far from the modern town of Nhulunbuy.

Thursday, February 17, 1803: On approaching I sent Lieutenant Flinders in an armed boat to learn who they were, and soon afterwards we came to an anchor in twelve fathoms, within musket-shot, having a spring on the cable and all hands at quarters. On the return of Lieutenant Flinders we learned that they were proas from Macassar, and the six Malay commanders shortly afterwards came on board in a canoe. It happened fortunately that my cook was a Malay, and through this means I was able to communicate with them. The chief of the six proas was a short elderly man, named Pobassoo. He said that they were upon the coast in different divisions sixty proas, and that Salloo was the commander-in-chief.

According to Pobassoo, from whom my information was principally obtained, sixty proas, belonging to the Rajah of Boni, and carrying one thousand men, had left Macassar with the north-west monsoon two months before, upon an expedition to this coast, and the fleet was then lying in different places to the westward — five or six together — Pobassoo's division being the foremost. These proas seemed to be about twenty-five tons, and to have twenty or twenty-five men in each. That of Pobassoo carried two small brass guns obtained from the Dutch, but the others had only muskets, besides which every Malay wears a dagger, either secretly or openly.

This image depicts a Macassar Trepanging Camp at Raffles Bay, Coburg Peninsula NT. It was painted between 27 March and 6 April 1839. The painter was Louis Le Breton, on a voyage of exploration under the command of French captain, Dumont D'Urville. Courtesy: NT Library

The Marion Sleigh

A ship like this steaming up Gulf rivers would raise a few eyebrows these days, but in the early 1900s the Marion Sleigh was a regular sight carrying supplies as far up as the Roper River Bar, and Borroloola on the Macarthur. The Marion Sleigh was of 506 tons burden, had a number of cabins for passengers, and often carried Darwinites who wanted a taste of adventure.

The Marion Sleigh bringing supplies to remote Gulf communities.
(Photo: Mataranka Museum)

On one trip in 1926, a troupe of young ladies on a pleasure trip were forced to endure ten days stuck on a Macarthur River sandbar, followed by serious engine trouble, and finally a storm near Groote Eylandt that saw the Marion Sleigh almost founder several times.

The Marion Sleigh was sold in 1932, her engines converted to diesel, and she spent her final years in New Zealand waters.

The Paddle Steamer Providence

Twin fireboxes, once attached to the Providence's boiler, still lie on the banks of the Darling near Kinchega Station.

The year was 1872, and for twelve months the 78-foot-long wooden paddle steamer Providence, under the leadership of Captain John Davis, sat on a waterhole north of Menindee waiting for the Darling River to rise. Drought had tightened its grip across western NSW and dried the river to a series of pools. Not even a rowboat could get through.

Finally, rain fell upriver, far away on the Balonne, the Macintyre, the Gwydir and the Namoi. As the river rose the Providence and her crew ambled downstream again, stopping at Menindee to load 200 wool bales and for a much-needed night on the town. The journey was paused for a night of riotous drinking and celebration at Maiden's Hotel.

The next morning, the crew, much the worse for wear, stoked up the firebox again, but neglected to check that the boiler had water. Around ten miles downstream, on a bend near Kinchega Station, the pressure reached catastrophic levels.

To say that the boiler exploded is an understatement. It tore the ship apart in a storm of flying metal fragments. The captain, engineer and stoker were all killed. The cook was blown into a treetop, and survived long enough to be rescued before dying of his injuries. Another young man had both legs broken and though Menindee's Dr Cotter tried desperately to save him, he also died. Henry Trevorah, a miner from Adelaide who had joined the boat at Menindee, was one of the few survivors.

A first-hand account, posted by a crew member of another paddle steamer from Kinchega Station in the days after the tragedy, gave the following account:

"We had been wooding last night between 6 and 7 o'clock, and had just got under steam again when the captain called my attention to the large quantities of painted boards that were floating down, remarking that he supposed a collision had taken place between two of the boats. The Ariel was just ahead of us, and the Providence was expected down. We picked up a cabin window, a door, and a large quantity of boards, also a swag containing some clothing, a little money, and a pin. We steamed on for about a couple of hours, and when we arrived at (Kinchega Station), were at once greeted with the shocking intelligence that the boiler of the Providence had burst and blown the vessel to pieces.

"Four of the hands on board were missing, while four others were saved — one, however, with a splintered leg and a gash in his arm, from which, the doctor is doubtful whether he will recover. This morning after breakfast we walked up to the scene of the disaster, about a mile from the station. The scene you must imagine, for I cannot describe. The banks were strewn with boards and debris of all kinds; while high up in the neighbouring trees were lodged pieces of timber, bedding and rugs, firewood, etc. A bag of flour was thrown over the tops of trees, and landed about 70 yards from the bank of the river, while a sledge hammer and several heavy pieces of casting were carried to an incredible distance. The wreck is lying in the middle of the river with her stern down stream. The appearance she presents is of being broken in two, the after part lying on top of the bow, one portion of the fore part being visible."

BY THE SAME AUTHOR ...

Whistler's Bones
by Greg Barron

At the age of fifteen, Charlie Gaunt signed on with drover Nat Buchanan. Two years later he joined one of Australia's greatest cattle drives – the Durack family's epic journey from Cooper's Creek, Queensland – to the Kimberley. Charlie came of age in cattle camps across the north and was both a participant in, and eyewitness to, a bloody conflict. Based on a true story, Whistler's Bones is an unprecedented adventure, a passionate love story, and both a celebration of the good things in the settlement of Northern Australia, and a damning indictment of the bad.

get it at ozbookstore.com

Camp Leichhardt
by Greg Barron

Ben Mulligan is a cop from the Northern Territory town of Katherine, with more than his share of problems. When he heads down to Camp Leichhardt, a Grey Nomad camp on the Roper River, to fish and get away from the stresses of life, he finds that all is not what it seems.

Ben uncovers a criminal conspiracy that will destroy lives and wreak havoc on local communities. With the beautiful Malea as his ally, he has to face his past head on, and tackle a cartel intent on making money at any cost. Yet, in doing so, he risks everything, even his own future.

get it at ozbookstore.com

OUTLAW: The Story of Joe Flick
by Greg Barron

When anthropologist Robert Morris arrives at the old Doomadgee Mission, at Bayley Point near Burketown in 1934, he's intent on learning local languages and customs. One very old woman living there, he discovers, was originally from outback New South Wales, and is something of an outcast amongst the Waanyi and Gangalidda locals.

On delving deeper, Morris discovers that the old woman was the 'wife' of a white stockman for more than thirty years in the frontier days, and claims to be the mother of one of the north's most notorious outlaws. Determined to record the facts of her son's crimes from her perspective, he sits with her each afternoon.

This is the story she told …

Get it at ozbookstore.com

Red Jack and the Ragged Thirteen
by Greg Barron

They called her Red Jack, for her hair was as bright as an outback sunset, hanging to her waist from beneath a stained cattleman's hat. On her jet-black stallion, Mephistopheles, she roved the north in the 1880s and 90s. Where did she come from, and where did she go? No one knows for sure, but the mystery lives on.

The Ragged Thirteen were a band of thirteen larrikins who put their stamp on Australian folklore with their devil-may-care journey across the wild Northern Australian frontier. They were not bushrangers, but were certainly inclined to bend the law. This fictional account is based on the recollections of settlers and pioneers, but is, most of all, a yarn in the best traditions of the word.

Get it at ozbookstore.com

www.ingramcontent.com/pod-product-compliance
Lightning Source LLC
Chambersburg PA
CBHW071903290426
44110CB00013B/1256